# *Morality*
## AND
# *Situation Ethics*

by

DIETRICH and ALICE
VON HILDEBRAND

*PREFACE BY*
**BERNARD HÄRING**

FRANCISCAN HERALD PRESS
Chicago, Illinois 60609

MORALITY AND SITUATION ETHICS, copyright 1966 by Dietrich von Hildebrand, Library of Congress Catalog Card Number: 66-25648. Published by Franciscan Herald Press, 1434 West 51st Street, Chicago, Illinois 60609. Made in the United States of America.

NIHIL OBSTAT:
    Mark Hegener O.F.M.
    *Censor Deputatus*

IMPRIMATUR:
    Most Rev. Cletus F. O'Donnell, D.D.
    *Vicar General, Archdiocese of Chicago*

May 25, 1966

"The Nihil Obstat and the Imprimatur are official declarations that a book or pamphlet is free of doctrinal or moral error. No implication is contained therein that those who have granted the Nihil Obstat and Imprimatur agree with the contents, opinions, or statements expressed."

Dulci Sorori
In Jesu Dilectissimae
Elisabeth Brewster von Hildebrand

# PREFACE

THE BOOK of my esteemed friend Dietrich von Hildebrand entitled *True Morality and its Counterfeits* was heralded when it first appeared as the most fully considered answer to a law-defying situation ethics as well as to an ossified legalistic ethics. The book is a positive and constructive answer. The reader can understand with little difficulty the basic principles in question.

Today the book takes on even more importance in the face of the emotional discussions about "contextual ethics" and above all in the light of the newly published book by Fletcher entitled *Situation Ethics*.

Even though it is far from me to deny the genuine concern of the advocates of "contextual ethics," I nevertheless believe that to a great extent there is in their utterances not only a misconception concerning basic laws but — and this is more deeply fundamental — a misconstruing of the order of love. To many, love is something vague and indefinite.

God is love. God is also truth. A love that seeks to honor Him must seek the truth, the genuine form, the meaningful expression in moral living.

I believe that the discussion about all these questions can be made more fruitful if it is conducted on the level of value-ethics and by means of careful phenomenology instead of merely in the categories of law, norm and context. Dietrich von Hildebrand does just that in a masterly way in this book.

Vatican II is calling to all to distinguish the unchangeable from the changeable forms. Only in this way can we make full use of the possibilities of salvation offered in the present hour. If beyond the changeable norms of the Church's directives, we see the values whose protection is the real issue at stake, then it will be easier for us to recognize the full continuity of life in the Church.

BERNARD HÄRING

## ACKNOWLEDGMENTS

I wish to express my indebtedness to the Rockefeller Foundation for the generous help they have granted me toward the completion of this work.

I also wish to express my grateful appreciation for the cooperation given me by Fordham University, in particular for lightening the many burdens connected with the routine of classwork. This has enabled me to finish my work much sooner.

Again I have to acknowledge a great indebtedness to my beloved friend and colleague, Dr. Robert C. Pollock, Professor of Philosophy at Fordham University, Graduate School, who has given so much care and time to revising my manuscript in a way in which only he is capable. The peerless help that he has given me presupposes many rare qualities: the capacity of attaining a most intimate understanding of the thought and intention of another philosopher; a great, loving respect for the ideas and style of another, and an understanding that they are basically inseparable; the humility to efface his own strong philosophical personality to such an extent that not the slightest note of his own style and way can be detected in the changes that he has suggested.

It is a great happiness to me to acknowledge publicly these hidden qualities in Dr. Pollock, which explain and account for what is by no means hidden: that he is both a great historian of philosophy and an eminent philosopher.

DIETRICH VON HILDEBRAND
*Professor of Philosophy,*
*Graduate School,*
*Fordham University*

*New York*
*Conversio Pauli, 1955*

# CONTENTS

*Preface*   vii

*Introduction*   3

*Chapter I.* The Pharisee   13

*Chapter II.* Self-Righteousness   22

*Chapter III.* The Tragic Sinner   36

*Chapter IV.* Letter and Spirit   50

*Chapter V.* Freedom of Spirit   63

*Chapter VI.* "Felix Culpa"   81

*Chapter VII.* Person and Action   87

*Chapter VIII.* Sin Mysticism   93

*Chapter IX.* The Christian Attitude toward Sinners   114

*Chapter X.* Basic Errors of Circumstance Ethics   130

*Chapter XI.* Christian Morality   155

*Appendix.* Allocution du St. Père à la Fédération Mondiale des Jeunesses Féminines Catholiques   171

*Epilogue.* The Case Against Situation Ethics   181

# *Morality*
### AND
# *Situation Ethics*

# INTRODUCTION

*"What I am going to say may startle you, but I think it's better to be a dirty beast than to have Brigitte Pian's brand of virtue."* [1]

A STRIKING feature of many modern novels, in contrast to the literature of former times, to a work like Manzoni's, *The Betrothed,* for instance, is the fact that roles seem in some way exchanged. Whereas in former times, the saint was opposed to the sinner, or at least the converted sinner to the mediocre man, now the sinner assumes the role of the hero, and the virtuous man is often presented as self-righteous, pharisaic, mediocre, or at least unamiable. In short, he is presented more or less as the negative counterpart.

This applies to several works of the great French writer, Mauriac, and to a certain extent also to Evelyn Waugh's novel, *Brideshead Revisited.* Above all, this characteristic is to be found in Graham Greene's novels. The glorification of the sinner is to be found in a much more exaggerated way, and with a completely different accent, in novels such as those of Jean Genêt.

This feature is more than a mere manifestation of a love for the complicated, the uncommon, the paradoxical. The motives for it are not of an artistic nature. It also goes definitely beyond the declaration of war on mediocrity that we find in Léon Bloy's powerful and volcanic novels. This trend is in reality a very significant symptom of a moral mentality widespread today, even among pious Catholics aiming at a deep religious life.

[1] François Mauriac, *The Woman of the Pharisees,* translated by Gerard Hopkins (New York: Henry Holt & Co., Inc., 1946), p. 75.

In an allocution to the Fédération Mondiale des Jeunesses Féminines Catholiques, His Holiness Pope Pius XII condemned this new ethics whose main features are characterized in the following terms:

The distinctive mark of this morality is that it is in fact in no way based on universal moral laws, for instance, on the Ten Commandments, but on the real and concrete conditions or circumstances in which one must act, and according to which the individual conscience has to judge and choose. This state of things is unique and valid but once for each human action. This is why the supporters of this ethics affirm that the decision of one's conscience cannot be commanded by universal ideas, principles, and laws....

In the determination of conscience, the individual encounters God immediately and makes up his mind before Him, without the intervention in any way of any law, any authority, any community, any cult or confession.

Here there is only the "I" of man and the "I" of the personal God; not of the God of law, but of God our Father, with Whom man must unite himself in filial love.

Viewed in this way, the decision of conscience is a personal risk, according to one's own knowledge and evaluation, in all sincerity before God. These two things, conscientiousness and the sincere response, are what God considers; the action does not concern Him....

All this corresponds perfectly to the "majority" status to which man has attained, and, in the Christian order, to the filial relation which, according to the teaching of Christ, has us pray: "Our Father." This personal view spares man from having at every instant to consider whether the decision to take is in conformity with the paragraphs of the law, or with the canons of abstract norms and regulations; it protects him from the hypocrisy of a pharisaical faithfulness to the law; it protects him as much from pathological scrupulousness as from levity or the lack of conscience, because it makes the entire responsibility before God rest personally upon the individual Christian. So speak those who are preaching the "new morality." [2]

---

[2] *L'Osservatore Romano*, April 19, 1952.

## INTRODUCTION

It is the merit of the great German theologian, Karl Rahner, S.J., to have been the first to lay his finger on this new ethics, which plays a great role in contemporary youth movements and literature.[3] He distinguished two different trends, "circumstance ethics" and "sin mysticism." He mentions no names and quotes no authors. He simply characterizes the two tendencies. They manifest themselves in various forms today, especially among Catholics. They are not philosophical theories, but rather lived, existential approaches to moral problems.

We might ask ourselves how, even among Catholics, a trend could arise that contains such obvious errors. Rahner himself tends to explain it exclusively in terms of the instability and insecurity of our present epoch. But it does not appear likely that this can be done successfully.

Granted that "circumstance ethics" contains grave and disastrous errors and that its most advanced champions fall into radical subjectivism (and, as Rahner rightly points out, into moral nominalism), nevertheless, in many novels somewhat influenced by this trend and plainly concerned with its problems, we also find good and praiseworthy elements.

Circumstance ethics is partially inspired by a reaction against a "heresy of ethos," which can be found in many mediocre, conventional Christians. It is the same heresy of ethos we have mentioned in several other books.[4] It is not a formal heresy. Those Christians infected by it do not depart from any dogma. But their entire approach to the supernatural sphere is conventional. Their obedience to Holy Church does not differ in quality from their loyalty to a profane authority. Their approach to the sacred commandments of God does not differ in practice from their approach to conventional rules of society concerning good manners, although they will theoretically admit a difference between them. They not only lack completely the *sensus supranaturalis*,

---

[3] *Stimmen der Zeit*, February, 1950.
[4] Cf. Dietrich von Hildebrand, *Menschheit am Scheideweg* (Regensburg: Habbel, 1954).

but they have no living relation either to the breath of the Holy Gospel or to the Liturgy or the Holy Church. Worldly standards have crept into the moral code by which they live. They bow before great efficiency. Success makes too great an impression on them. They differ in no way from nonbelievers in their attitudes unless a strict moral commandment intervenes. They have lost even a faint awareness of the words of Christ:

"If you were of the world, the world would love what is its own. But because you are not of the world, but I have chosen you out of the world, therefore the world hates you." [5]

Cardinal Newman says of these Catholics:

... the world then witnesses against you by being good friends with you; you could not have got on with the world so well, without surrendering something which was precious and sacred. The world likes you, all but your professed creed; distinguishes you from your creed in its judgment of you, and would fain separate you from it in fact. ... [6]

... your sole idea of sin is, the sinning in act and in deed; sins of habit, which cling so close to you that they are difficult to detect, and manifest themselves in slight but continual influences on your thoughts, words, and works, do not engage your attention at all. You are selfish, and obstinate, and worldly, and self-indulgent; you neglect your children; you are fond of idle amusements; you scarcely ever think of God from day to day, for I cannot call your hurried prayers morning and night any thinking of Him at all. You are friends with the world, and live a good deal among those who have no sense of religion.[7]

The origin of circumstance ethics and of sin mysticism is certainly linked to a reaction against this bourgeois, conventional deformation of Christianity.

The "heresy of ethos" manifests itself also in a relative in-

---

[5] John, 15:18–20.
[6] Cardinal Newman, *Discourses to Mixed Congregations* (London: Longmans, Green & Co., 1891), p. 165.
[7] *Ibid.*, p. 162–163.

dulgence toward pharisaism and self-righteousness. It cannot be denied that in the conscience of the average Christian the danger of pharisaism plays less of a role than the danger of concupiscence. In many Christian societies, self-righteousness does not evoke scandal to the same degree as adultery or drunkenness do.

Circumstance ethics reacts further against the tendency to substitute legality for morality, to replace moral values by *rights,* to adapt morality to the juridical sphere, and to make of the juridical sphere the *causa exemplaris* of morality—a tendency that can be found among many Christians and sometimes even in Christian textbooks.

In some adherents of circumstance ethics, one also finds a protest against an overemphasis on actions seen in an abstract light, implying a disregard of the individual's entire personality, with its different strata and its mysterious complexity. It is a protest against oversimplifications that we often encounter in moral judgments of Christians concerning their neighbors.

Circumstance ethics fears a kind of depersonalization that easily goes hand in hand with the above-mentioned tendency of adapting morality to the juridical sphere. It is believed that in order to escape from this oversimplified and stereotyped approach, one must stress the uniqueness of every single case— a uniqueness arising not only from the circumstance but also from the uniqueness of every individual person. Existential or circumstance ethics thus claims that our moral decisions cannot be ruled by abstract, general principles and commandments, and at the same time accents the point that the complexity and uniqueness of every concrete situation require a personal decision of our conscience.

It is certainly true and in full conformity with the Christian tradition to say that knowing that somebody has never committed murder, theft, or adultery, we only know of the absence of grave moral sins, but still remain ignorant of what kind of man he is from the moral point of view. He may be a highly virtuous person or an uncharitable, proud, hardhearted man. Even when we are aware that he gives a great deal of money for charitable purposes and that he attends mass every Sunday, we as yet do not have evidence of his moral character.

In order to learn something about a person's moral standard, we must first of all ascertain his motives for abstaining from evil actions, for almsgiving, or for going to church on Sunday. To use traditional terms, we have to examine the *finis operantis,* and not only the *finis operis.* To use our own terminology, we must recognize not only that he has abstained from evil actions, and that he has realized goods having a morally relevant value, or accomplished actions that, as such, are morally good; we must know also whether or not his will was motivated by the morally relevant value or by a moral commandment.[8]

This applies, however, only to judgments concerning either good actions or the omission of evil actions. In the case of the performance of an evil action, it must be said that the violation of certain moral commandments definitely informs us of a moral evil. In realizing that someone has committed adultery or murder, we know unquestionably that he acted immorally and that he is stained with a moral disvalue. But as long as we are not acquainted with his motive, the *specific* moral disvalue of his action has not yet disclosed itself. The fact, as such, only reveals that he acted immorally, but the degree of his immorality, the specific moral disvalue of his action, depends also upon his motives.

There are, however, some moral commandments that have not the character of an absolute "veto," which may be superseded by a *higher* obligation. Such, for instance, is the obligation to keep a promise or to fulfill a task that is entrusted to us. These formal moral obligations may be suspended by the call of higher-ranking goods, for instance, the moral or physical emergency of another person. Such a case is given when someone bound by a promise defers its

[8] Dietrich von Hildebrand, *Christian Ethics* (New York: David McKay Company, Inc., 1953), Chapters 17 and 19.

fulfillment because he hears the cries of a man in extreme distress.

In such cases, we do not even know whether someone acted rightly or wrongly as long as we only know that he did not keep his promise. It may even be that his action was especially good. Yet we have to emphasize that the full moral picture requires in all cases the knowledge not only of the nature of the intent,[9] but also of all the attendant circumstances, the past life of the person, his education, psychic health, and so on. These elements, though not determining the quality of the moral value, nevertheless hint at the person's degree of responsibility and the symptomatic function of his action in relation to his entire personality.

There are, moreover, concrete prescriptions that have the character of advice to avoid situations that could become morally dangerous. In hearing that someone has placed himself in such a situation, we definitely do not know whether his doing so was morally wrong or not. It may be that it is a symptom of his having done something immoral, or it may be at least an indication of his thoughtlessness and carelessness. But it may also be that serious reasons motivated his action, which may, therefore, not be symptomatic of anything morally negative.

In these cases, obviously the knowledge of mere *appearances* does not justify any moral judgment. Here the moral datum is still completely indefinite. Something immoral may be at stake, but it may also be that the attitude is morally unobjectionable or even morally good.

Finally, it may be that not even an ambiguous situation is in question, but merely something shocking in the frame-

---

[9] In saying "intent," which traditionally is expressed by *finis operantis*, many factors that have a bearing on the moral value or disvalue of an action or an attitude are tacitly implied. First, whether or not a knowledge of the object's morally relevant value or disvalue is given. Second, the clarity and depth of this knowledge; third, the motive, i.e., whether or not our will is a value response; fourth, whether it is a pure value response or a response also motivated by something subjectively satisfying, and several other factors. Cf. *Christian Ethics,* Chapter 17, p. 349.

work of certain traditions, for instance, a young girl's being seen alone on the street with a young man. This is considered shocking in certain countries or in certain epochs, and in others not at all so.

Here nonconformity to the mere customs of a local tradition has no moral significance whatever.[10]

We want to broach the entire subject matter, extending from the most definite situation resulting from the conformity or nonconformity with a prescription, principle, commandment, rule, to the completely morally insignificant one. This will give us the opportunity of separating the chaff from the wheat in circumstance ethics, and, above all, of seeing the all-important role of general moral commandments and the impossibility of doing away with them.

But there is still another reason for enumerating different cases. The moral judgments of the pharisees and of the self-righteous people, against which circumstance ethics is especially directed, are precisely characterized by the fact that they tend to treat these five different cases we have mentioned as being on one and the same level.

If we wished first to stress the shortcomings against which circumstance ethics rightly protests, we must now emphatically say that the thesis that circumstance ethics proposes as a solution is basically wrong. Moreover, it is necessary to point out that besides the positive motives, there are motives behind this movement that are of a completely negative character, such as the unfortunate idol of "freedom" and the desire to throw off the burdensome yoke of morality.

Sometimes we even find traces of the attempt to throw off our creaturehood.[11] Furthermore, a very prominent

---

[10] There is always the possibility, of course, of eventually giving scandal to one's "weak brethren" (*scandalum pusillanimorum*), which should obviously also be taken into account from the moral point of view.

St. Augustine says: "It is nothing to the City of God what attire the citizens wear, or what rules they observe, as long as they contradict not God's holy precepts...." *The City of God,* XIX, 19, p. 256.

[11] D. von Hildebrand, *The New Tower of Babel* (New York: P. J. Kenedy, 1953), p. 10 ff.

motive is the idea that man is entitled to be completely happy on earth, and connected with this is the desire to find a solution for all cases in which morality and divine commandments require a sacrifice of earthly happiness on our part.

In speaking of circumstance or existential ethics and of sin mysticism, we must, however, constantly recollect that it is not a philosophically formulated theory, but rather an intellectual movement, finding its expression in several youth organizations and in literature, for example, in the novels of François Mauriac, Graham Greene, Gertrud von Le Fort, and many others.

It is thus less a theory than a trend, whose extent varies greatly. The authors representative of the trend as a whole differ greatly concerning the point to which they push their ethical thesis. Gertrud von Le Fort goes further than Graham Greene. The latter goes much further than Mauriac. The passages quoted by the Holy Father and referred to previously go further than what we find in these novelists, for they come close to denying the validity of all general moral commandments.

In our appreciation and criticism of circumstance ethics, we shall therefore sometimes refer to the more mitigated forms of it, sometimes to the more radical. A certain positive appreciation will apply only to more mitigated varieties, certain criticism only to those that are radical.

Our aim is to combine two different tasks. One is to do justice to the elements in circumstance ethics that are valuable contributions, following the principle, *"ex stercore, aurum"* (gold from the dunghill). The other is to refute in detail the disastrous errors that circumstance ethics and sin mysticism embody, errors that have been condemned by the Holy Father. Both tasks will serve our ultimate goal of a clearer elaboration of Christian morality.

Rahner distinguishes clearly in his article between circumstance ethics and sin mysticism. They are definitely two different trends according to their theoretical content, constituting, from a philosophical point of view, completely different theses. But since, in an existential trend as expressed in literature and certain youth movements, both are interwoven, we shall not always be able in our criticism to separate them in a clear-cut way.

Circumstance ethics and sin mysticism pretend to a large extent to represent the truly Christian morality. In their fight against pharisaism, they often introduce themselves as champions of the Christian spirit, by opposing to a merely natural morality the mystery of the cross and the mystery of grace.

Refuting this pretension of circumstance ethics, we also hope to throw some light, therefore, on the specific character of Christian morality.

In order to understand all the moral problems underlying circumstance ethics, we shall begin with an elaboration of pharisaism in all its forms.

*We want to point out emphatically from the very beginning that when we speak of sin, we in no way imply that a mortal sin is necessarily at stake. To commit a mortal sin presupposes not only the gravity of a violated commandment, but also several conditions in the agent, such as clear knowledge, full responsibility, and others. In no way do we intend to make any theological statements.*

We are restricting ourselves to the moral problem and use the term "sin" and "sinner" in the sense of an objective discrepancy in relation to moral commandments, and the presence of attitudes embodying a moral disvalue and an offense against God objectively implied in it. We also prescind from the question of the presence or absence of sanctifying grace in given cases.

## Chapter I

## THE PHARISEE [1]

PHARISAISM is one of the most refined forms of pride. The satanically proud man [2] wages war against all values. He wills to deprive them of their "metaphysical throne." Like Lucifer, he hates God and wants to dethrone Him. The pharisee, on the contrary, seeks the satisfaction of his pride by adorning himself with "moral perfection." The pharisee bows before a God, but a God deprived of His infinite holiness and His divine, inscrutable mystery. He admits a God, but only a God with mere formal absoluteness. He really loathes the quality of the divine. He hates infinite love and holiness.

The satanic type of man fights against God and all values. The pharisee is more subtle. He does not formally wage war against values, not even against moral values. Yet he hates true morality and substitutes for it a merely legalistic and ritualistic morality. He wants to relish his piety and goodness, to glorify himself before a merely formal God. He identifies his cause with God's cause, instead of making God's cause his own. He is incapable of any true value response. The possession of moral values, as he understands them, is a mere means for the satisfaction of his pride. His *ressentiment* is directed neither against the important-in-itself [3] nor against a formal conception of God. It is directed against the divine, against God's authentic Holiness. This duplicity gives pharisaism the character of hypocrisy. But it

---

[1] Our analysis of the pharisee is concerned with a classical moral type. We are not attempting an exegesis of the historical pharisee.
[2] Cf. *Christian Ethics*, p. 442 ff.
[3] Objective values in their formal aspects.

is not the normal hypocrisy of a Tartuffe,[4] who cynically disguises himself as a saint in order to deceive other persons and attain his egoistic aims.

The pharisee's hypocrisy is much deeper and more refined than Tartuffe's. Tartuffe is a plain, sanctimonious swindler. He puts on a show of sanctity intended to deceive other persons for the sake of his profit and inordinate desires. The pharisee aims at more. He is not content with a mere appearance of morality, whose only function is to dupe others. He wants actually and not only ostensibly to sit on the throne of morality, but a throne of morality regarded as a mere ornament and means of self-glory.

Pharisaic hypocrisy implies no discrepancy between mere appearance and reality, but rather between true morality and a desubstantialized, formalistic morality. This kind of hypocrisy implies a falsification of morality as such, not only the conveying of a false impression of one's character. Thus the pharisee is, in a certain sense, really endowed with this pseudo morality. At least he is himself convinced he possesses it. Therefore, instead of cynically playing a role before others, he relishes his correctness. He plays this role not only in front of other persons as Tartuffe does, but even before himself and before God.

Tartuffe is, moreover, not primarily dominated by pride, but rather by concupiscence. The make-believe holiness and the admiration that it commands are mere means to his profit. They do not really satisfy his pride. The pharisee, on the contrary, is not a swindler like Tartuffe. He seeks satisfaction of a deep metaphysical pride and this by "abusing" God and moral values. He needs God for his glory, yet at a distance, and a God so formalized that no real confrontation can take place between his soul and the true world of God. Such a confrontation would be unbearable for him and would unmask his intrinsic falseness. Though the pharisee needs the moral sphere for his glory, it is only a desubstantialized and legalized morality at which he aims. True

---

[4] The main character of Molière's comedy entitled *Le Tartuffe*.

morality, especially Christian morality, is unbearable to him, and he hates it.

Pharisaism implies an existential hypocrisy, a constitutive hypocrisy. The pharisee is possessed by the spirit of the lie. The pharisee described in the gospel is mainly preoccupied with the ceremonial of the law. He is an enemy of the "mystery" of God. He ignores the "spirit" everywhere and reduces everything to the fulfillment of the letter. For him, the scandal of scandals is the Incarnation, the Epiphany of God, the "intrusion" of God's infinite holiness in the world of his own pseudo theology.

Abiding by the letter, which is so deeply characteristic of pharisaic falseness, must be clearly distinguished, however, from an analogous tendency proper to the mere functionary with his red tape. The metaphysical bureaucrat, for whom the serious things in life are wrapped up in juridical formulations, who believes everything that is inaccessible to juridical categories to be more or less a nebulous romance, is a dull and fossilized type. In no way, however, does he embody the deep, poisonous pride and hypocrisy and the hatred of all true goodness characteristic of the pharisee. The shrinkage of the world resulting from the bureaucrat's reduction of it to his categories is primarily a symptom of mediocrity, dryness, affective sterility. Many moral faults and a good portion of pride and concupiscence may naturally intervene as well. The bureaucrat is rather ridiculous, boring, depressing, but one does not find in him, as in the pharisee, an abyss of subtle and refined hatred of light, and such a complete absence of all goodness, bounty, and charity.

Cleaving to the letter on the part of the ritualistic bureaucrat also has a thoroughly different character. He overrates ceremonial laws. In his naïveté, he has an excessive regard for the letter. He has, nevertheless, a truly reverent attitude, and his devotion has a content of real service. He may be a prisoner of the letter and thus may underestimate and ignore the spirit, but his cult of the letter bears no immanent hostility toward the spirit.

For the pharisee, on the contrary, the stress laid on the letter is a means both of fighting the spirit and of feeding his self-glory. There is no character of service in it whatever. The appalling character of the pharisaic attitude and its innermost falseness disclose themselves clearly as soon as we realize that the ceremonial law, which is essentially a service, is being abused as a means of self-glory.

Up to this point the analysis of the pharisee has been restricted to his peculiar, ambivalent attitude of formal zeal for God and hatred of God's infinite holiness as revealed in Christ.

We must now turn to a further analysis of the quality of pharisaic pride, especially to an analysis of the pharisee's attitude toward his neighbor.

We have stressed in other works [5] that pride increases in proportion to the rank of the value that is used as a means for one's self-glorification. The real antithesis to humility is self-glorification in moral values and not the relishing of physical beauty, titles, a high position, intelligence, or artistic gifts. Pharisaism is the climax of this most poisonous moral pride.

The pharisee's attitude is possible only in a human creature. Cain's pride is diabolical and is primarily to be found in the fallen angel, Lucifer. Pharisaic pride, however, presupposes a human world and even a religious tradition. It is a form of pride that can unfold itself only in a specific situation. In the framework of the specifically human forms of pride, pharisaism is the most refined and the deepest, exhibiting the most hideous aspect of human pride. It is surpassed only by the satanical pride of a Cain, which is, as we saw, not exclusively or primarily human.

The pharisee is characterized by a specific form of hardheartedness that is even more repulsive than the hardness of a cruel and ruthless despot like Genghis Khan. It poses as the

---

[5] D. von Hildebrand, *Transformation in Christ* (New York: Longmans, Green & Co., 1948), Chapter 7, pp. 139–41; *Christian Ethics*, Chapter 35, p. 445.

voice of justice and adorns itself with the shield of right and of moral correctness. A tyrant's hardness is the hardness of passion, of brutality, of injustice. His judgment is often an expression of his arbitrary mood. Pharisaic hardness, on the contrary, leans on the "sword" of morality; it is the hardness of pseudo justice. In "judging" sinners, the pharisee holds aloft the "sword" of morality, but of a morality that he has voided and deprived of its intrinsic goodness.

The pharisee embodies the very antithesis to charity to a far greater extent than a man who completely falls prey to his passions of ambition, lust of power and lechery, for example, a brutish monster like the Father Karamazov. These "monsters" are much less consistent than the pharisee. They may suddenly be capable of surprisingly human attitudes, such as compassion or generosity. They may be so without abandoning their basic, evil attitude. The pharisee, who is self-controlled, rational, who bases his hardness not on brutelike passions, but on a pseudo morality, is much more consistent in his hardheartedness. In his attitude, the abyss of rational, self-righteous, cold hardness is revealed. It is the terrible void of an absolute absence of charity in those to whom our Lord says: "Woe to you, Scribes and Pharisees, hypocrites! because you are like whited sepulchres, which outwardly appear to men beautiful, but within are full of dead men's bones and of all uncleanness. So you also outwardly appear just to men, but within you are full of hypocrisy and iniquity." [6]

We can now understand better why the pharisee embodies the very antithesis to charity. True, we also find the very antithesis to charity in the satanically proud man, but he embodies likewise an antithesis to justice and to every moral value, in fact, to every value as such. The pharisee, on the contrary, in his pseudo justice, embodies a specific antithesis to charity.

The pharisee is further characterized by his enjoyment of a sense of moral superiority. "O God, I thank thee that I am

[6] Matthew, 23:27.

not like the rest of men...." [7] The pharisee gloats over the moral failures of others: they confirm his own moral superiority. Joy over other people's moral failures is not to be found in the same way in other forms of pride. The satanically proud man also rejoices at immoral actions of other persons, but for another reason. These immoral actions are not a springboard for his own moral superiority, but he sees in them a triumph of evil, a victory in his war waged against God. His joy over another person's fall—and the keenness of his joy is in proportion to the moral excellence of the other person—does not differ in its quality from what he experiences in his own wicked acts. It is the same joy that he experiences at any rebellion against God, and at any offense against Him, whether accomplished by himself or by others.

The pharisee, on the contrary, rejoices over the moral failure of his neighbor because he makes it a steppingstone to his own moral superiority. He uses it as a means for the satisfaction of his pride, which, precisely, is centered on moral superiority or, rather, a pseudo-moral superiority.

Another type of proud man, the despot craving for power, does not rejoice in the moral failures of others. He does not care about their moral status, granted that they obey him and remain willing instruments in his hand.

Nor does the specifically vain man rejoice in the moral failures of another person. He does not need the moral failures of other persons in order to feel himself superior, for he is too convinced of his own superiority, too exclusively engrossed in his own goodness, beauty, and wisdom.

Like the pharisee and the satanically proud man, the mediocre immoral man also rejoices when he witnesses failures in morally noble people. Yet his joy has a completely different function and character. He rejoices because he finds an excuse for his own sins in the failures of other persons. In no way does he feel morally superior to them, but his bourgeois conscience is allayed by the fact that he can say: "You see, other people do the same thing. After all, it

---

[7] Luke, 18:11.

is impossible to expect so much. Man is weak." Here the moral failures of other persons serve not as a source of satisfaction in one's own moral superiority, but as a consolation for one's own moral inferiority.

The mediocre immoral man does not elevate himself above other persons. He draws other persons down to his own level. Consequently, his joy does not have a proud, self-complacent, and self-righteous character or a cold hardness. It is rather a vile justification of one's own moral "mess," a specific joy of exoneration and alleviation.

Sometimes people rejoice, witnessing the immorality of other persons, because of the satisfaction of finding company in the realm of immorality. The general human desire for companionship is perverted, leading the person to rejoice at finding companions in moral weaknesses, vices, and aberrations. The source of this joy makes bad company disastrous. Apart from the danger of seduction, bad company tightens the fetters of vice.[8] One is "sheltered" by company. One rejoices in evil tendencies shared, in being understood by another, in not being condemned or reproved by him, in being able to glide downward undisturbed. Deplorable as this joy is of finding company in evil-doing (a joy that, by the way, is restricted to evildoers dominated by concupiscence and is not to be found among the different classes of sinners who are bound by pride), it not only clearly differs from the pharisee's joy over the moral failures of other persons, but it is also much less wicked. It has more the character of weakness and is not antithetical to charity, although it is incompatible with it. Pharisaic joy over the moral failures of other persons, on the contrary, is the very antithesis to charity. It embodies the deepest indifference toward the welfare of other persons, the coldest disinterest in their true welfare.

---

[8] It is the opposite analogy to that of our striking roots in the field of moral goodness through community with morally noble persons. In the above-mentioned case, one strikes new roots in the realm of moral evil through company with evil persons.

A further characteristic of the pharisee is that, in order to attain his selfish ends without staining himself, he even induces other persons to do evil. He wants to use the evildoer for his own aims, but in a way that does not disturb his consciousness of moral correctness and pseudo justice. Again he abides by the letter and finds a solution that—according to the letter—leaves him without blame and nevertheless provides for the satisfaction of his hatred, his revenge, his selfish interests. The Pharisees incited the people of Israel to clamor for the crucifixion of Christ, and they wanted Pilate to impose the death sentence.

The specific refinement and ambiguity characteristic of the pharisee disclose themselves in this procedure. He uses other persons—the evildoers—whom he looks down upon as sinners, in order to attain for himself an end that he could not attain directly without staining himself morally. He does evil, hiding himself behind the letter, by which he thinks he can remain morally "intact" and "pure." He satisfies his evil passions and preserves his consciousness of moral correctness.

The pharisee tries, as it were, to void morality of all charity, even of the form of charity that is to be found in true justice. He attempts to borrow from true morality the unique humiliating power inherent in the moral verdict, and to use it as a weapon for his pride. He abuses the "metaphysical throne" of moral values, the objectively "strong" position of the morally good in order to crush his neighbor in a way in which only moral blame can crush. He tries to isolate the "judge" character of morality from all the intrinsic goodness of morality so as to profit by the moral sword in his campaign of pride, all the while fighting against God *in the name of orthodoxy.*

The pharisee is above all characterized by the absence of mercy or, more precisely, by a spirit that is the very antithesis of mercy. Perhaps the antithesis of mercy is still more typical in the pharisee's case than the antithesis of charity. It comes to the fore in the pharisee's rigidity, disguised in the cloak of right and justice. The rigidity of pseudo justice, with its worship of the letter and its "judgelike" character, is the very antithesis of mercy.

The pharisee hates mercy. He does not want to appeal to God's mercy,[9] but only to his own merits. He refuses mercy to other people and uses the rigid scale of the letter in order to condemn them. Thus the words of our Lord, *"Misericordiam volo et non sacrificium"* [10] (I desire mercy and not sacrifice) are the very death sentence pronounced upon pharisaism.

[9] St. Augustine, *De Libero Arbitrio,* translated by Francis E. Tourscher (Philadelphia: Peter Reilly Co., 1937): "And what is more unworthy of mercy than the unhappy man who is proud—too proud to accept mercy." P. 313.
[10] Matthew, 9:13.

CHAPTER II

SELF-RIGHTEOUSNESS

WE HAVE briefly analyzed the characteristics of the pharisee proper, the pharisee condemned by our Lord in the parable of the Pharisee and the Publican and on many occasions. Now, let us turn to certain derivatives of pharisaism, to certain mitigated forms of this perversion. Let us analyze the various types of self-righteous people.

There is a type of self-righteous man whom we may call the self-righteous zealot. He may have a sincere desire to obey God and to avoid offending Him. Yet in doing so he feels himself to be morally correct and relishes his correctness.[1] He looks down on the sinner in a hard and indignant manner. He experiences a certain joy, witnessing the moral failures of other persons, because he finds it pleasurable to be indignant at immorality. It will occur to him to have doubts about the legitimacy of this pleasure. Yet of him, too, it can be said, as Mauriac says of Brigitte Pian in his book, *The Woman of the Pharisees,* that she always managed to find "some reason that would make her pleasure seem legitimate and fit it into the pattern of her moral perfection." [2]

Looking at a repentant sinner, the self-righteous zealot relishes playing the role of a merciful, compassionate person. After crushing a sinner under the weight of his indignation, he enjoys condescendingly lifting him up again in a gesture of sham mercy. This gesture also serves, however, to confirm

---

[1] François Mauriac, *The Woman of the Pharisees*: "She was a logical-minded woman who kept to a straight road marked out by clearly labeled principles. She never took a step that she could not immediately justify." P. 81.
[2] *Ibid.,* p. 80.

the abyss separating him from the sinner.³ His morality has a sour quality about it. He lives on the *qui vive* in order to detect immoral actions of other persons. He may feel some contrition about the moral failures in himself that do not make him topple from the pedestal of his self-righteousness. His examination of conscience takes place only within the narrow frame that his pride has constructed. As a result, he never experiences a true and deep contrition, that "breakthrough" before God, that full surrender to Him, in which one abdicates one's own pride, falling as a naked beggar into His loving arms. The self-righteous zealot is not disposed to admit his faults before other persons, except when this acknowledgment can be used as a means of proving to himself and to others his own humility.

He always possesses a good portion of that haughtiness which we described in our book, *Transformation in Christ*.⁴ He shuns feeling dependent upon other persons, experiencing indebtedness by gratitude. In short, he abhors occupying an inferior position in relation to others. He dislikes looking up to any other person or submitting to anyone other than those having God-given authority. Yet even with respect to the latter, he adopts a critical attitude. He feels himself entitled to judge their individual life and personality. He even enjoys finding some traits in them that call for a "reluctant" criticism. He always assumes to himself the position of one offering final judgment.⁵

The self-righteous man we are speaking of even feels himself to be guilty if he does *not* "judge" other persons. He may believe he represents and defends God's cause, but in fact he enjoys his role of judge and his own moral superiority: "... there are some people who choose God, but ... perhaps God does not choose them." ⁶ Though in his own life he does

---

³ *Ibid.*, p. 26.
⁴ Cf. Chapter VII, "Person and Action."
⁵ "...she regarded it as her privilege to watch over every soutane that came within her orbit." Mauriac, *op. cit.*, p. 83.
⁶ *Ibid.*, p. 75.

not necessarily abide by the letter as against the spirit of moral commandments, he will do so with respect to others. Although he may have an idea of Christian morality for his *own* person that surpasses the mere letter, in judging *other* persons, he will abide strictly by the letter.

The mind of the self-righteous zealot incessantly revolves about moral questions. He is continually indignant, continually scandalized.

One of the most typical characteristics of this self-righteous man is his readiness to judge another person's actions and general behavior without ever taking the trouble to determine the real motives and all the specific circumstances attached to the case. He deems it sufficient to know *that* someone failed to conform to a moral commandment in order to pronounce moral sentence upon him. Consequently he handles all the different cases mentioned before [7] as being on one and the same level. When he hears that someone's behavior might be *symptomatic* of something immoral, he will feel fully justified in indignantly condemning that person's behavior as if he already had valid *proof* in his hands that the actions in question were unquestionably immoral.[8]

Even if someone's "crime" is merely a violation of local social tradition, the self-righteous zealot will respond with full-fledged moral indignation, the more so if an act that shocks society can *in any way* be related to indecency.[9]

The self-righteous zealot will always tend to suspect the worst in other persons' moral conduct. He will always presuppose a sinful conduct of life rather than a virtuous one, and will always anticipate his neighbor's prospective fall.

When his expectation turns out to be true, he will be highly satisfied, apart from his general satisfaction with others' moral failures. Should the future, however, not con-

---

[7] Cf. Introduction, p. 8 ff.

[8] "Gracious Heaven! what worse could they do than kiss?" Mauriac, *op. cit.*, p. 75.

[9] "I was too ignorant as yet about love to have noticed that my stepmother could never approach the subject calmly, but that as soon as it was mentioned she became, as it were, all worked up." *Ibid.*, p. 16.

firm his predictions, should a person prove to remain on the path of the Lord, the self-righteous zealot will resent it. He prefers to see the other fall rather than to have wrongly predicted his fall. He is characteristically opinionated and unshakeable in his opinions.

One of the most hideous features of the self-righteous zealot is his abuse of particularly sublime Christian virtues. When he is rightly blamed by someone, he will neither respond with fury nor admit his fault. He will play the part of the individual, unjustly attacked, who, for the sake of Christ, generously forgives the wrong done to him.

From the very beginning, he will falsify the entire situation, "meekly" offering the other cheek, to receive "patiently" new, unjust offenses. He will thereby disarm the one who rightly has blamed him and will succeed in shifting the theme of the situation. Though he obviously has wronged the other person, he will twist the situation into an occasion for exhibiting his Christian spirit of forbearance.

This attitude embodies an infamous hypocrisy. The self-righteous zealot wants to avoid an objective admission of his fault or error. Unlike the obstinate, proud man who attacks the one who blames him and responds with fury, however, the self-righteous individual disguises his unwillingness to admit his being wrong, his proud obstinacy, and his opinionatedness in the garments of sublime Christian virtues. He succeeds with his disguise by forgiving when there is nothing to forgive and by offering willingly to God the pretended cross of being misunderstood and misjudged. He generously forgives where he should be asking for forgiveness, and where above all, he should admit his fault.

If once he were to beg for forgiveness, however, he would do so in a way that would never include admission of his error or a yielding in the conflict. He will accuse himself only of having failed to fight in the right manner or of having been overpowered because of his zeal. In his opinionatedness, he will never give up any position, never admit being wrong in his intention. He will only ask forgiveness for being too violent in his procedure. He will, moreover, accuse himself in such an extravagant fashion and will "humiliate" himself to such an extent that he will disarm the other person and even force the other person to elevate and praise him.

This last feature, namely the exaggeration referred to, is to be found not only in the self-righteous zealot. It is a very widespread, half-conscious trick used to disarm anyone who rightly blames us. It is to be found in most persons in a more innocent form, as a kind of escape, a ruse of man's nature. It leads one to say, "My fault is terrible, unpardonable," in an exaggeration by which he reverses the situation to such an extent that the person he has wronged is called upon to console him. Yet this escape has a radically different character from that of the self-righteous zealot's hypocrisy. It is a kind of *"captatio benevolentiae"* and in no way a show of humility as it is in the self-righteous. It is a rather infantile trick used to escape blame and all the disagreeable things connected with it. But with the self-righteous zealot it is quite otherwise, for he anticipates "being elevated" before God and before himself and other persons through a sham humiliation.

The infantile type of exaggerated self-accusation is similar to a trick used to silence the well-deserved blame of a friend. Someone blamed by a friend says, "I have always known and said that I am a hopeless, miserable sinner and that you waste your time on me. I have always said that you cannot love me on account of my utter unworthiness." The friend who hoped to give him a fraternal correction to help him to overcome his fault is now forced to give it up and to begin to console him, assuring him that he is, on the contrary, a lovable person and that this fault has no significance whatever.

Something analogous is to be found in Dickens's *David Copperfield* when Dora's tears succeed in frustrating David's attempt at educating her. In this case, however, it has rather the character of a "spiritual strike."

To return to the self-righteous zealot, he is, as we can see, tainted with some of the features of the pharisee. Yet he clearly differs from the true pharisee, in whom the gesture of self-complacency and self-glory takes place in a much deeper stratum. In the pharisee, self-glorification is the basic and innermost attitude. It poisons his entire relation to the moral sphere and to God and fills him with the spirit of the lie. In the self-righteous man, the same attitude does not display itself at the same depth and thus does not affect his entire moral life. In him, the possibility of a sincere, general will to be morally good is not yet stifled, and on certain occasions we may find him assuming many a single, noble attitude. His basic moral attitude is not perverted to such an extent that it can no longer be endowed with any moral value. It is only corroded. This corrosion is a perversion, but still within the framework of moral goodness. The perversion of the full-fledged pharisee places him definitely outside this frame. It locates him within the frame of plain moral wickedness.

We must clearly distinguish the self-righteous *mediocre* man from the self-righteous zealot. He is a type that is much more common than the zealot. He is the man in whom there is no deep moral striving, who wants to be morally "in order," so he can consider his life as "morally unobjectionable." He wants to be in conformity with moral commandments. Yet he tends to view them in the light of legal prescriptions. Unlike the self-righteous zealot, who does not necessarily stand by the letter in regard to himself, he will be quite content with the letter in regard to himself and will not trouble himself about the spirit. He wants to be dispensed from experiencing a real consciousness of man's sinfulness. He will certainly not deny it on a theoretical level and as a general statement concerning *all* men. But he wants to escape a real confrontation with God. He knows nothing about the experience that led St. Peter to say, "Depart from me, for I am a sinful man...." [10] He wants to be dispensed

[10] Luke, 5:8.

from conscious actualization of man's metaphysical situation, from the *"se humiliare"* that every deep, true contrition implies. He attempts to escape it not by moral indifference, as does the morally wicked man, the debauchee, the criminal, or the enemy of God, but by remaining in conformity with the letter of moral commandments and thereby ensuring himself against feelings of moral insecurity. He is far from being a zealot and his mind is far from revolving incessantly about moral questions. He has not the moral acidity typical of the self-righteous zealot. On the contrary, he wants to pursue his private interests undisturbed—business, politics, science, family concerns, and so on. He wants "moral security" and "intactness," not primarily in order to relish them as the self-righteous zealot does, but in order that he may render to God what he *has* to render to Him, and to be able then to dedicate himself fully to "Caesar," that is, to his private life and its more or less selfish interests.

The mediocre correct man shares with the self-righteous zealot the habit of judging others' moral failures in a superior and hard way. He has not the "exalted" indignation of the zealot. He does not live on the *qui vive* concerning immorality. But he also enjoys his own correctness, and, from its secure level, he, too, judges "sinners" in an apodictic and superior manner. Together with the self-righteous man and the pharisee, he feels no solidarity whatever with the sinner. Certainly, no one should experience any solidarity with sin, but, when faced with the fall of one's neighbor, every man should be reminded of his own moral frailty. Everyone should fear that he himself may fall, and should be aware that, had God's grace not protected him, he could have fallen as low.

The *self-righteous,* mediocre man, however, is not to be identified with everyone who is morally mediocre. He is not the man who has just a mediocre conception of morality and who minimizes all moral commandments to such an extent that they become acceptable to a mitigated pride and concupiscence.[11] Nor is he the man who has an "average" morality, the tepid, lukewarm man who is neither really good nor really bad. He is rather the *correct* mediocre man, whose mediocrity is combined with self-righteousness, with the desire of feeling himself to be correct. He abides strictly, and not tepidly, by the letter of moral commandments. Yet he abides by the letter alone, not by the spirit. He exhibits a moral hardness that not every mediocre person possesses. On the contrary, the tepid, average man is jovial and very tolerant of other persons' moral failures. As we saw before,[12] he rejoices about them only in order to alleviate his own conscience. But the self-righteous mediocre man's joy over the moral faults of other persons has the same connotation as that of the self-righteous zealot. It also derives from relishing one's own correctness and superiority when confronted with the sins of others.

With the self-righteous zealot, he also makes no distinction in his moral condemnation between the immoral action proper and the mere symptoms of a possibly immoral action. Whether dealing with true moral principles or with rules of conduct merely recommended by cautiousness, or with principles pertaining to local customs only, these two types of self-righteous men place them more or less on the same level and under the title: *"One does not do such things."*

The self-righteous man further considers all manifestations of morality and religious ardor not listed in his moral code as exaggerations and symptoms of unhealthy exaltation.

This feature is especially developed in the mediocre, correct man. He feels disturbed by any manifestation of the true breath of Christian charity and humility. His correctness and mediocrity are challenged by it. As long as these manifestations remain at a distance that does not force him to have to confront his life with this spirit, they will not bother him. As long as they are found in the lives of canonized saints —whose lives he will not read anyway—he will abstain from

---

[11] Cf. "compromise type" in *Christian Ethics*, p. 417 ff.
[12] Cf. Chapter I, "The Pharisee," pp. 18–19.

any judgment out of respect for the Church. This respect however, is not true reverence for the Church as the Mystical Body of Christ, as the heavenly Jerusalem, as possessed of its infallible magisterium. It is rather loyalty to the Church viewed as an undisputed pillar of the society in which he traditionally lives—as the pregiven frame of the "society of the *bien pensants.*"

For the self-righteous, mediocre man, the real norm is whether or not something is fit "for good society." A man whose religious and moral life carries elements capable of shattering the world built up by conventions and public opinion and the norms of bourgeois decency appears to him as exaggerated and unhealthy.

Mauriac brilliantly describes this mentality in his novel, *Vipers' Tangle,* when Hubert writes to his sister:

> This religious exhibitionism of his amounts only to a criticism, direct or oblique, of the principles in which our mother brought us up from childhood. If he indulged in a murky mysticism, it was only that he might use it as a stick to beat that rational and moderate faith which has always held a place of honour in our family. Truth is poise. *(La vérité, c'est l'équilibre.)* [13]

If he accidentally becomes acquainted with some deed or certain traits of the saints that confront him with the "folly of Christ," with the "two-edged sword of the word of God," "extending even to the division of soul and spirit," he will shrink back and turn away, saying, "The saints also have sometimes exaggerated."

But when he is confronted with extraordinary Christian traits in a living person, he will openly despise him and consider it as bad taste and unpleasant exaggeration. He not only looks down on the sinner, but also on the "exaggerated" piety, which he considers shocking.

The moral "ardor" of the mediocre, self-righteous man,

---

[13] François Mauriac, *Vipers' Tangle,* translated by Gerard Hopkins (London: Eyre & Spottiswoode, Ltd., 1952), p. 204.

displays itself in the negative direction only, in the rigidity of his judgment of sinners. For himself, on the contrary, he will be content with a minimum, with a correct observation of the letter, insofar as strictly obligatory moral and religious precepts are in question. Nor do we find any ardor in his response to extraordinary virtues in other persons. There is no proportion between his negative rigidity and his positive mediocrity.

This applies primarily—as already mentioned—to the self-righteousness of the mediocre, correct type. But even the self-righteous zealot has a tendency to consider heroic, extraordinary manifestations of the spirit of Christ as exaggerated. Though he has no minimalist attitude in his own moral life, though he is not mediocre, he still pours more ardor into his indignation over "sinners" than into his veneration for saints or into his response to extraordinary manifestations of the Christian spirit. When he is confronted with the breath of Christian charity and of Christian freedom of spirit in his neighbor, he will view them with suspicion and even be scandalized as soon as they interfere with his disposition to pass sentence upon sinners.

But in spite of the fact that the two types of self-righteous men share several traits in common with the pharisee, traits that poison and pervert their morality, they still clearly differ from the real pharisee. Indeed, there is a yawning abyss between them and such a man. As we saw before, self-righteous men do not have his fundamental attitude of pride, his basic hatred of God's infinite goodness and holiness. The God they worship is not a purely formal one, deprived of His divinity. Their perversion displays itself within the frame of morality itself and on the basis of a positive moral attitude. It is not a form of antimorality as pharisaism is in fact. They do not share the hypocrisy and falseness of the pharisee. They are not basically and thoroughly wicked.

Although in individual cases it may be difficult to determine whether a man is a pharisee or only self-righteous, it is of the greatest importance to make the distinction. It would be a grave injustice to consider the self-righteous and the mediocre, correct men as real pharisees. It would further distort the entire problem of the moral superiority of the noble sinner with respect to a certain type of correct man. That the real pharisee ranks morally lower is not difficult to see. It is only after having made a clear distinction between the pharisee on the one hand, and both the self-righteous zealot and the self-righteous mediocrity on the other, that we are able to reach the real problem underlying circumstance ethics. We must now set aside the pharisee and concentrate on a comparison of the two types of self-righteous men with the tragic sinner.

There is, however, still another type of man, who, although he abides by the letter of moral commandments, greatly differs from the three above-mentioned types. He has no pharisaic feature whatever. He is the timorous man, who lacks freedom of spirit and who has more a servile fear of God than a filial fear of Him. He sincerely wants to obey God, and he has the general will to be morally good, but he lives in a constant state of fear and is looking for confirmation that will assure him that he is on the right path. He will never dare to make any decision without being backed up by the letter of moral prescription. He will never have the courage to follow God's call when it manifests itself in a special situation through the values at stake alone, but only when it is backed up by a formulated prescription. In a certain way, the timorous man is the very opposite of the above-mentioned self-righteous mediocre man. Though they both abide by the letter of moral prescriptions, the timorous man does it because he fears to offend God. He does not restrict morality to the letter, but he always wants the reassurance of the letter.

The mediocre, correct man, on the contrary, wants to save himself the trouble and discomfort of feeling himself to be a sinner. He is eager to fulfill the letter of the prescription for the sake of attaining this aim and for the satisfaction of the pride that he feels in knowing himself to be "correct." The letter of the prescription has here the character of a *minimum,* whereas in the case of the timorous man, it has the character of a *maximum.* Notwithstanding this antithesis and the completely opposite motives leading to their respective abiding by the letter, they are nevertheless both antithetical to the true Christian freedom of spirit. The timorous man, although incomparably superior to the mediocre, correct man from a moral point of view, exemplifies an antithesis to the saint, insofar as he does not seek peace of conscience in the imitation of Christ, in a loving confidence in God, in the loving delivery of himself and abandonment to God, in faith and hope, but rather in exterior criteria, in the "letter of the law." By that he ultimately attempts to escape from a real confrontation with God and from the "risk" of getting into such a depth. He is satisfied to substitute formulas for this deep confrontation. He is looking for a guarantee of his conformity with God without taking the risk that a decision based exclusively on a full moral intuition implies, a decision based on the spirit of a moral commandment, though possibly in contradiction to the letter of that commandment.[14] His case is somewhat analogous to that of the man who always wants an extrinsic guarantee of truth, which he may use as a "bridge of asses," instead of having the courage to grasp a self-evident truth in a direct insight when he is faced with it.

The timorous man also shares with the three afore-mentioned types the characteristic that his judgment about other persons is orientated to the letter of the commandment instead of to its spirit. He will not judge them "from above." He will not manifest any hardness. Still less will he rejoice in any way over his neighbor's moral failures. But he will shrink from anyone who offends the letter of a moral prescription. He will be scandalized in the sense of the *scandalum pusil-*

---

[14] As we shall see later, servile and timorous obedience to the letter of the law may in a particular case lead one to go clean against the intention of the legislator.

*lanimorum*. His moral timorousness will prevent him from abiding by any measure other than the letter.

There are many different nuances within the frame of this moral timorousness, ranging from spiritual laziness to a typical scrupulousness. The latter is clearly the milder form of the two, morally speaking. Although the different types of moral timorousness are clearly distinguishable from the self-righteous type, whether zealot or mediocrity, they also are antithetical to the true Christian freedom of spirit.

We lay stress on the "abiding by the letter" that is due to moral timorousness, because circumstance ethics also contains a protest against this attitude, without, however, clearly distinguishing the type of man involved from the others, the pharisee, the self-righteous zealot, or the self-righteous mediocre man. This protest comes to the fore in the emphasis it places on "personal risk."

In their fight against general moral commandments, the champions of circumstance ethics lay great stress on "personal risk," as they call it. Since the timorous man shuns taking any personal risk, he is also included in the general attack launched by circumstance ethics.

We shall see later on how disastrous in effect is the interpretation of the freedom of the children of God offered by circumstance ethics. Abiding by the letter of a commandment instead of by its spirit is certainly wrong, but it effaces neither the validity of general commandments nor their indispensable role in our moral life. It does not even cast suspicion on the "formulation," that is, on the letter as such. The fact that the spirit is expressed in the letter has a great value, a value that is not invalidated by the fact that abiding by the letter while ignoring the spirit is a thoroughly wrong attitude.

It is not the fault of the commandment or of its formulation, if, instead of taking the spirit as the real measure, someone abides by the letter in an insipid way, sacrificing the spirit in order to preserve the letter. We shall see later on that it is only in extraordinary cases that, in order to follow the spirit of the commandment, we must contradict the letter.

It would be quite wrong to believe that breaking with the letter is, as such, something either indifferent or even, to a certain degree, positive. Normally, the letter and the spirit are in agreement. It is only in extraordinary cases that they contradict each other.

CHAPTER III

## THE TRAGIC SINNER

CIRCUMSTANCE ethics claims that a sinner may love God more than the self-righteous, whether zealots or mediocrities. In many novels we can find the following antithesis: on the one hand, the self-righteous man who observes all the moral commandments, and on the other, the sinner who, though in conflict with one or several moral commandments, is more charitable, more humble, more true, and more sincere than the self-righteous man with his hypocritical virtue.

Circumstance ethics goes even further. For it sometimes claims that a sinner may be morally superior even to a mediocre, morally correct man who is not self-righteous—superior as a personality, more disposed to a real conversion and to a real love of God and neighbor. Although the correct man abstains from grave sins, he may lack all positive virtues. He may be conventional and dull, ignoring the real moral drama of mankind and, consequently, according to circumstance ethics, inferior to certain sinners.

Before entering into a discussion of the conclusions that the champions of circumstance ethics draw from this antithesis, we must analyze the type of sinner whom they regard as superior. It is clearly not the diabolically wicked man, such as Cain or Iago.[1] Nor is it the man who cynically disregards all moral commandments, such as Richard III; nor the ruthless proud sinner, such as Don Rodrigo[2] or Don Giovanni.[3] It is primarily the sinner who is aware of his sin and regrets it and who suffers because he is separated from God.

[1] In Shakespeare's *Othello*.
[2] One of the main characters of Manzoni's *The Betrothed*.
[3] Main character in Mozart's opera of the same name.

Only such a sinner is regarded as having a greater love of God than the self-righteous man or the merely mediocre one.

We must, however, not only exclude many types of sinners who, because of the gravity of their sinning and their basically sinful moral attitude, cannot simultaneously be aware of their sinning and regret it. We must also exclude sinners who because of their good moral status bear no relation to the problem that has arisen in circumstance ethics. Among such we have, first of all, the converted sinner. Conversion and God's pardon create an utterly different situation. The sinner has risen from his fall. The screen separating him from God has fallen. We need only think of the good thief and of the words addressed to him by Christ.[4]

We are concerned with the man who in sinning is fully aware of what he is doing and regrets it, although he cannot muster the strength to give it up. Such may be the case, for instance, when a Catholic has contracted a marriage with a divorced woman. He is aware of his sin and suffers because he is separated from God. Yet he has not the courage to break up with her. On the one hand, he knows that if he were to do so, it might crush her completely and throw her into utter despair. On the other hand, he loves her so much that he lacks the strength to separate himself from her. Yet he is fully aware of his sin and deeply suffers as we have said, because he is separated from God. According to circumstance ethics, he may still love God, and he may be charitable and humble.

Or let us take the case of a drunkard. He began drinking in order to forget a great sorrow. He sought an escape. But with time, drinking became a habit, even a passion dominating him. He is fully aware of his sin. He is deeply humiliated by his vice. He hates it, but he is too weak to overcome it. This man may still love God, and he may be charitable and humble, although he commits something objectively sinful.

The sin we are concerned with must have a truly tragic

---

[4] "Amen I say to thee, this day thou shalt be with me in paradise." Luke, 23:43.

character. In the case of an invalid marriage, the sin is tragic only when a mutually deep and ardent love is in question. The sin can be called "tragic" only if renouncing this marriage would mean an ordeal implying a crucifixion of hearts, and what would therefore be tantamount to a renunciation of earthly happiness.

If someone should marry a divorced person because of financial interests or social advantages, the sin committed would not be tragic, but obviously ignoble. Such despicable motives exclude the possibility that the sinner while fully experiencing his sin, really suffers from the kind of conflict just described. Awareness of the sinfulness of his action and deep sorrow over it are the distinctive marks of the tragic sinner. In the case of the drunkard or the man who is the prisoner of a passion that he is too weak to overcome, noble motives, it is true, are not to be found. But the tragic character is here rooted in the fact that his sinful passion overpowers him—thus the sinner can really hate his sin and deeply suffer from it, though lacking the strength to overcome it.

Although in each case (the man who marries a divorced woman and the drunkard), the motives clearly differ in their quality and rank, in both instances the awareness of sinfulness and deep sorrow over it may be found. This characteristic is, as one can easily see, the element that separates the tragic sin from the ordinary sin.

It must, however, be stressed that in speaking of a tragic sin, we *in no way* intend to imply that there is any moral trial in which a man is objectively bound to fall. We want to point out emphatically that the term "tragic" bears no connotation whatever that this sin is unavoidable or that it is excusable. It only indicates a special type of sin springing from weakness rather than from real wickedness.

A completely different type of sinner who is morally noble notwithstanding her sin, is Sonja in Dostoievski's novel *Crime and Punishment*. She sells herself to save her family from utter misery. She sins by doing something objectively impure and by co-operating with the sin of others. But her sinning carries the intention of making a terrible sacrifice in order to help others. She does not yield to a passion, nor does she choose something immoral, moved by human, noble motives, or as a result of a clash between a noble objective good for herself and a moral commandment. On the contrary, she considers her action as a great sacrifice, implying the surrender of her most precious objective good. For the sake of saving other persons, she is doing subjectively just the opposite of what the tragic sinner does. Whereas the tragic sinner acts in contradiction to a moral commandment in seeking something for himself, either a great objective good for himself [5] or the appeasement of a passion, Sonja apparently chooses the morally good and sacrifices a high personal good. She sins, however, because what she sacrifices is not only a high objective good for herself, but something that is God's in a special way,[6] and in any case, her sacrifice is morally forbidden. She overlooks the fact, moreover, that in doing so she co-operates with the sin of her partner, whose evil act clearly implies both a sinful *finis operis* and a sinful *finis operantis*.

Sonja is not value-blind in the normal sense of the term. She sees the value of purity and the disvalue of impurity. In this respect she is, therefore, pure. She would never do something impure for the sake of satisfying a passion. The very fact that her action is experienced as a supreme sacrifice tells us clearly that she is not impure. But the idea of a supreme sacrifice blinds her and leads her to overlook the fact that there is more at stake than an objective evil for her, namely, something objectively sinful, and objectively and subjectively sinful insofar as her partner is concerned.

The question arises as to how much she is responsible for her sin, which is in a peculiar way mixed with a specifically

---

[5] Cf. *Christian Ethics*, notion of objective good for the person, p. 49 ff.
[6] D. von Hildebrand, *In Defense of Purity* (New York: Sheed & Ward, 1935), Chapter III.

moral intention. It is a very unique case of moral error, definitely differing from the various types of moral value-blindness. But it *is* a moral error, and she cannot be exonerated from all moral guilt. Something is morally wrong in her. Otherwise she could not overlook the objective sinfulness of her deed. But it is an uncommon case, in which the readiness to sacrifice her happiness out of charity blinds her to the sinfulness of this very sacrifice. In this case, patently, a high moral standard and a deep love of God coexist with this objective sin. It is much easier to understand the coexistence here than in the case of the tragic sinner. The incomparable moral superiority of Sonja over a self-righteous, correct man is evident. In her case, it is not only that nobility of character can be found notwithstanding her sin, but a morally sublime act is subjectively interwoven with her objective sin.

It is of the utmost importance, however, to understand that, notwithstanding all the positive moral elements included in her attitude, she commits a sin. The highest moral intention can never do away with the objective sinfulness of her deed. All the charity invested in this sacrifice cannot compensate for its immorality. It remains true that we have to deplore her way of acting, though we may be deeply touched by her noble charity and heroism.

Sonja's case is especially illustrative for several reasons. First, it concerns the danger of an exalted heroism that believes that to sacrifice oneself for others is *in any case* morally good and pleasing to God. It is part of the widespread error that the harder something is for us the more noble it is.[7] In contradistinction, however, to the ideal of "duty" in the Kantian sense, with its arid, hard, stoic quality, there is here an overstressing of altruistic heroism as such, a danger of "exaltation," which overlooks the fact that a great objective good

---

[7] Henri Bergson is quoted as having said: "The moral rule which appears to me the highest and most fruitful is to choose of two duties the one that costs the more." (Floris Delattre, *"Les Dernières Années d'Henri Bergson,"* Revue Philosophique. Nos. 3, 8, March, August 1941, p. 138.

for me may also have a morally relevant value that definitely forbids my sacrificing it. In the sacrifice here in question one arrogates to oneself a sovereignty that is incompatible with *"religio."* [8] This sacrifice implies the arrogation of a right we do not possess as creatures. It implies an irreverence and disorder similar to the case in which someone offends God out of "charity" for a human person.

Secondly, this case is especially instructive because it reveals the moral impact of the *finis operis* and shows clearly that the noblest intention based on a moral error cannot save and cleanse the objective immorality of certain acts.

Yet it is not the type exemplified in Sonja but the tragic sinner, who circumstance ethics claims is in the final analysis endowed with a deeper love of God and with more humility than the self-righteous, correct man.

This antithesis, however, is ambiguously formulated. Self-righteousness is a horrible, moral disvalue. It also offends God in a specific way. There is a certain equivocation in calling the "tragic sinner" a sinner, and the self-righteous individual, whether zealot or mediocre correct man, a "nonsinner." In truth, he also sins through his self-righteousness, by his hypocritical pride, which affects and even falsifies his entire moral life. It is a vice that is more difficult to circumscribe, which is less accessible to clear-cut moral commandments, but it is in obvious antagonism to charity and humility and thus implies a specific offense against God. Instead of opposing the "sinner" to the self-righteous, we should rather say that the sin of self-righteousness is more grave, a deeper offense against God, a greater separation from God than the sin of the tragic sinner. It is, above all, a sinful *"habitus"* pervading the entire moral life of a person—not a single, sinful deed or an isolated vice. Moreover, it is accomplished without awareness of its sinfulness. Clearly this does not mean that here a type of ignorance is in question that would in any way suspend responsibility. It is, on the contrary, the kind of blind-

---

[8] Cf. *The New Tower of Babel*, p. 11 ff.

ness for which we are fully responsible.⁹ And in this case, it is even not so much a blindness for the disvalue of self-righteousness as such, but rather a closing of one's eyes to one's *own* self-righteousness. It is the typical case of self-deception, in which one succeeds by disguising the satisfaction of vicious trends under the cloak of virtue. As a result, the self-righteous man looks upon himself as especially virtuous whereas, as we have seen, the tragic sinner is aware of his sinning.

Self-righteousness is especially hideous because it corrodes all positive moral attitudes, whereas the "tragic" sinner can be generous and charitable and can do many morally positive things, notwithstanding his sinning. The vice of self-righteousness, on the contrary, is like a poison that affects every domain of the moral life, and poisons especially all virtues and good actions.

Thus it is quite true that the tragic sinner may still be better than the self-righteous man, not because of his sinning, but because his sin is less grave and does not corrode in the same way the entire life of the individual as self-righteousness does.

The superiority of the tragic sinner over the sinner who is self-righteous discloses itself when we think of the following elements.

In the tragic sinner, we can still find the metaphysical seriousness of morality. Though he is in conflict with the moral law, he still stands within the orbit of that true morality which extends into eternity. In his tragic fall, he still testifies to the "breath of the eternal," [10] which pervades true morality, because of his deep suffering, his experience of the weight of guilt. The tragic sinner stands in this "space,"

---

[9] St. Augustine says: "... but he that thinks he lives without sin does not avoid sin but rather excludes all pardon." *De Civitate Dei, The City of God*, translated by John Healey, Everyman's Library (New York: E. P. Dutton & Co., 1947), XIV, 19.

[10] Soren Kierkegaard: "The ethical is and remains the highest task for every human being. The ethical is the very breath of the eternal." *Post-Scriptum*, pp. 99-100.

not only objectively—this applies to every sinner—but subjectively as well. He himself is aware of the confrontation with God. His personality, therefore, is still in contact with the true world of God. Looking at him, we are drawn into the drama of true morality.

The self-righteous zealot, on the contrary, narrows the realm of morality and draws it down to a bourgeois level. The atmosphere that *his* morality gives forth is no longer filled with the breath of eternity. He surrounds himself with a morality deprived of its eternity dimensions, of its intrinsic breath-taking grandeur.

Clearly, he also stands objectively before God in the great realm of true morality. But subjectively he has severed himself from this realm. His ideal of morality is dry, rigid, and acid. It sets up a barrier hindering the light of true morality from pervading his mind.

If, seeing the tragic sinner, we are reminded of the great drama of man and our heart is attracted and moved by the intrinsic beauty of morality, if in our compassion for a sinner we experience all the misery of being banished from the *domus Domini* and, in the same breath, the intrinsic lovableness of moral goodness, it is quite otherwise in the presence of the self-righteous man. For in him morality appears as a narrow and depressing bondage. His very personality discredits morality. He himself has become a blind, shutting out the light of true morality.

All this applies also to the self-righteous mediocre man. He is, perhaps, to an even greater extent, like an opaque glass veiling the face of true morality. His mediocrity hinders the light of true morality from pervading his mind. In his presence we are in danger of seeing morality in a completely wrong light, and even of being disgusted by it.

Some champions of circumstance ethics, however, claim, as we saw,[11] that the tragic sinner not only may rank higher than the self-righteous man, whether zealot or mediocrity,

[11] P. 36.

but that he also may be morally preferable to a mediocre, correct man who is not self-righteous.

It is only here that the antithesis "sinner and nonsinner" may be made, although, in a certain sense, every man who is not a saint is a sinner. But the mediocre, correct man who is neither self-righteous nor in any sharp conflict with a moral commandment does not sin. He is not stained with moral disvalues, but he lacks positive moral values. Although he does not murder or commit adultery, although he goes to church on Sunday, his charity is very mediocre, and his personality does not possess real purity or humility. He will never do more than the letter of a commandment strictly requires. He is petty, conventional, more or less superficial, even incapable of any of the great human feelings. But with all his mediocrity he does not sin as the tragic sinner does. He observes the letter of moral commandments, but he does not understand the breadth, height, and depth of their "spirit."

It is not yet the moment to enter into a discussion about whether or not the "tragic sinner" ranks higher than a mediocre correct man. Perhaps it is true that many morally positive attitudes can be found in the tragic sinner that the mediocre correct man does not possess. What matters is to see that it is not the sinning that is responsible for the morally positive qualities, or the correctness that is responsible for mediocrity. The mediocre, correct man is morally poor and deficient in spite of his correctness. The tragic sinner possesses certain moral values in spite of his sin. To see any disadvantage in the absence of a glaring conflict with a moral commandment, is absurd. To view "correctness," in the sense of the absence of such a conflict, as a kind of superficial smoothness betrays both a blindness to the intrinsic ugliness of *every* sin—including the "tragic sin"—and to the intrinsic beauty and depth of innocence.

It is this sort of blindness that is at the bottom of the so-called *sin mysticism*. As in the intellectual field there exists a perversion according to which an interesting, complicated, intelligent error is preferred to a simple, evident truth, so there exists also a moral perversion that leads us to prefer the dramatic, interesting tension of a tragic sin to simple innocence. We shall come back later to the fundamental error of sin mysticism. Here it suffices to stress that the real moral inferiority of the "correct" man does not derive from the absence of a tragic, sinful conflict, but from his shallowness and from his lack of real humility and charity.

Yet it is not only the tragic sinner who has been contrasted with the self-righteous man. It is even the mean sinner, the avaricious, hardhearted, impure man, who, notwithstanding all these horrible moral disvalues, has, in the very depth of his soul, a longing for God—he whose heart is not really anchored in money and lechery, but thirsts for God's love, which he has not yet found. Such a man Mauriac opposes to the self-righteous, mediocre people whose hearts are really anchored in money and social standards, though they are correct Christians according to the letter.

Here the problem is a completely different one from that which is found in the case of the tragic sinner. It is no longer the discrepancy between on the one hand, habitual, noble qualities and a basically good direction of will and, on the other, the moral disvalue of an action, or the incapacity to live up to one's moral intentions in the sphere of action. Here habitual immorality, an evil character, and vices are contrasted with a hidden desire and longing. Thus the discrepancy in this case is between the real desire of the heart and the vices resulting from one's vain efforts to satisfy this desire with money, lechery, and fame. This type of sinner may —according to Mauriac—remain a prisoner of his vices especially because the self-righteous and mediocre Christians he has met did not make him acquainted with the true Christian spirit. There is also tragedy in these sinners, though of a completely different sort from that of the above-mentioned tragic sinner. The morally positive element in these sinners is much less discernible than in the tragic sinner. It is hidden, covered by repulsive vices, and, in a certain sense, only potential. Only someone with a loving, merciful heart, someone who approaches sinners in a truly Christian spirit, will detect this hidden noble desire, the *"cor inquietum donec requiescat in te."* [12] And he alone will be able to lead this desire out of the labyrinth of prejudices, bitterness, and passions in which it has lost its way.

Even this sinner may be preferable to certain self-righteous mediocre people who want to be in conformity with the minimum of moral laws, as it were, in order to be able to serve both God and Mammon. Yet, in this case nobody should try to derive from this antithesis any glorification of sin. Obviously it is in no way because of the sinning and the vices that this man may be preferable to the self-righteous correct man. It is, on the contrary, incredibly surprising that in spite of his moral squalor, he may still be preferable because of the underlying, deep noble desire. The stress lies here on the mystery in man's nature and on the difficulty of discovering his ultimate yearnings, also on the necessity of approaching the sinner in the hope of finding in him an underlying, noble desire. One emphasizes here that ostensibly correct Christians may in reality be lacking in any real love and longing for God, and may, moreover, be self-righteous, and consequently still greater sinners.

The lesson contained in Mauriac's novel *Vipers' Tangle* is that of making us aware of how easily we may be deceived in our moral evaluation of persons. It is exemplified in the paradox that even in a really terrible man there may live, in the very depth of his soul, a noble longing that may yet victoriously manifest itself despite the moral filth; and this very thirst places him above the self-righteous correct man.

We must add, however, that it would be a grave error to extend this evaluation to all sinners. Granted that we are never able to "judge" any sinner—including the pharisee—in the sense of imposing a final sentence, the pity that Mauriac invokes in the preface to his novel [13] is a pity of a

---

[12] St. Augustine, *Confessions* I, 1: "Our heart is restless till it rests in thee."
[13] *Vipers' Tangle:* "The man here depicted was the enemy of his own flesh and blood. His heart was eaten up by hatred and by avarice. Yet, I would

sort other than that which we must have for the immortal soul of every sinner, even of the most diabolical monster. Here it is a pity that does not apply to a Don Giovanni, a Don Rodrigo, a Richard III, a Father Karamazov, or a monster like Iago. It would be ridiculous to claim that a Don Rodrigo or a Richard III is preferable to a self-righteous, mediocre, yet morally correct man. They are obviously incomparably worse than the self-righteous correct man. It is a very special type of sinner in whom a noble thirst underlies all his perversion. But it is in no way allowable to apply the same attitude to the ruthless enemy of God who is filled with pride and concupiscence. The kind of sympathy due to the former would be inadequate with respect to the latter. Moreover, we must stress that also in the self-righteous, mediocre, correct man there is still a positive element that makes him far superior to the ruthless enemy of God. Granted that his mediocrity makes us despair, that his self-righteousness makes him repulsive, that the hypocrisy of disguising his egoism with garments of moral correctness and piety disgusts us, nevertheless, in his very correctness there still lives a faint respect for God and a feeble link to the moral law. With all our aversion, we should never wish that he would lose this remnant of obedience to God. We should, on the contrary, be glad that at least this positive element is still to be found. We should still feel the solidarity that unites us with him as against the gulf that separates us from the open, ruthless, moral monster. Our horror of his mediocrity must never make us unjust to him. This is a great danger in many noble minds, whose hatred of mediocrity makes them lose sight of the fact that sin is worse than mediocrity.

As for the self-righteous zealot, however, we must stress the

have you in spite of his baseness, feel pity, and be moved by his predicament. All through his dreary life squalid passions stood between him and that radiance which was so close that an occasional ray could still break through to touch and burn him: not only his passions, but, primarily those of the lukewarm Christians who spied upon his actions, and whom he himself tormented. Too many of us are similarly at fault, driving the sinner to despair and blinding his eyes to the light of truth." P. vii.

point that we may likewise find in him an underlying, frustrated noble thirst and desire. The sincere good will, the earnest striving for moral perfection that these self-righteous zealots often possess reveal the presence of a noble moral intention that has been perverted and distorted through several unfortunate experiences. Self-righteousness and acidity may in fact be the result of frustrations and deceptions. This does not mean that they thereby become excusable, or that they lose their character of being grave moral faults. This psychological origin does not take away one's responsibility. But it makes us realize that this self-righteous zealot also calls for our special sympathy. We may say, "What a pity that this person's good will, which the right spiritual director could have oriented to a high moral standard, has degenerated into such an odious perversion as self-righteousness." But here we may clearly see the noble basic moral attitude and the discrepancy between it and self-righteous hardness and moral acidity. In this type we may find something analogous to the case of the sinner mentioned before.

We have attempted to expound upon the data from which circumstance ethics starts. Its champions rightly stress the horror of self-righteousness and the emptiness of mediocrity. But apart from their unfortunate thesis, which claims the invalidity of general moral commandments,[14] behind their antithesis of the tragic sinner and the self-righteous individual and even the mediocre, correct man there lurks a disastrous tendency either to glorify [15] or at least to belittle sin.

[14] Cf. Chapter X, "Basic Errors of Circumstance Ethics."
[15] Cf. Gabriel Marcel, *Man against Mass Society,* translated by G. S. Fraser (Chicago: Henry Regnery Co., 1952):
I am thinking for instance of a play I propose to write in which we see a young married woman, all keyed up, confronting her husband, who is just about to play the host, with all the respect due to such a personage, to a rival and imitator of Mr. Jean Genet, with this question: "Tell me, Jo: can you swear to me that in the presence of Jacques Framboise, who has just come out of prison, you experience nothing that at all resembles a feeling of superiority"? Jo, confused and quite taken aback, remains silent. The lady presses her point: "Answer me, Jo: the whole future of our relations depends on your answer." In her discreet way, she then adds that Jo ought to feel a

Sin is even sometimes encouraged as a possible *"felix culpa."* Circumstance ethics further overlooks the fact that there are goods having a morally relevant value, the ignorance of which is always morally bad and illegitimate. No motive, however noble, can compensate for the disvalue of actions violating these goods.

Finally, its exponents arrogate to themselves the role of champions of the spirit of morality against a narrow abiding by the letter, not seeing that in many cases it is impossible to fulfill the spirit while departing from the letter. The following chapters will deal with these different errors. We shall begin with a clarification of the terms "spirit" and "letter" and an analysis of when and where we can fulfill the spirit though departing from the letter, or fulfill the letter though neglecting the spirit.

<hr>

little ashamed, if anything, of wearing the white flower of a, legally at least, blameless life....

If I have allowed myself a somewhat farcical digression here, it is to throw a clearer light on those generally inverted values which a contemporary literary *elite*—an international *elite*, too—is rapidly today tending to adopt for its own. And here, also we find conformism and "right-thinking persons." One would be judged a "wrong-thinking person" in such circles if one persisted in pointing out that theft, in itself, is a reprehensible act. Pp. 5-6.

## Chapter IV

## LETTER AND SPIRIT

In previous chapters, we referred several times to the antithesis of letter and spirit. It is necessary to analyze these notions more minutely. It is especially important to consider when and where, in relation to moral commandments, a distinction between letter and spirit can be made. Before discussing this problem, however, we must distinguish various meanings of letter and spirit.

We must first distinguish three formally different meanings. According to the first, the term "abiding by the letter" designates a failure to distinguish the essential from the non-essential in propositions, moral commandments, or precepts. Thus, in abiding by the letter, one clings to a mere formulation, to something accidental and exterior. This can be for very different motives, as we shall see later on, but the result is always the same—mistaking the surface for the content. "Spirit" here means the real meaning of the proposition or commandment, its essence and true intention.

By "letter" one sometimes refers to actions, and by "spirit," in the same context, to the underlying motive. A man who abstains from fornication because he is a misogynist, or gives money to the poor merely in order to make an impression, observes the letter of the commandment but fails to fulfill its spirit. Such a discrepancy of "letter" and "spirit" (in this second sense) is, as we know, quite common. Here, abiding by the letter assumes the character of a mere abstention or of acting in conformity with the commandment but without the moral motive and intention.

"Abiding by the letter" can also mean that one isolates a moral commandment, cutting it off, as it were, from the "living organism" of morality. "Letter" here means the isolated commandment, and "spirit" the spirit of morality as such, the "norm" of moral goodness, implying the hierarchy of values. Thus abiding by the letter in this case means to ignore all the self-evident restrictions of a commandment, restrictions arising from the fact that this commandment is overruled by a superior one, or because certain conditions dispense us from fulfilling this commandment. As for "spirit," it refers here not so much to the *real* meaning of a special commandment as opposed to an accidental detail of its formulation, but rather to the spirit out of which this commandment also ultimately flows and to all its implications. Hence, in this third case, to abide by the spirit means to co-operate fully with our conscience, to confront God in everything, and to take the trouble to examine all circumstances in the light of Christ's commandments in order to understand what God's will is in a particular situation.

In all three cases, "abiding by the letter" may frustrate real obedience to the commandment in question. In the first case it can do so by ignoring the very meaning of the commandment and abiding by mere nonessential details. In the second case it can be brought about by accomplishing something exteriorly and, as it were, accidentally, without the required motive, namely, the moral intention and the spirit of obedience. In the third case it can happen by falsifying the intention of the commandment, isolating it and neglecting all the implicit conditions of its application.

Having distinguished these three formally different notions of "letter" and "spirit," we shall now analyze various exemplifications of the different attitudes and motives that lead us to abide by the letter instead of the spirit.

First, there exists a naïve and foolish way of following the letter. It is exemplified in people incapable of grasping the real meaning of a statement or a precept. They do not understand the essential; they "miss the point." They register the letter only, getting stuck on the nonessential and accidental features of a proposition. This is often the case with simple people unaccustomed to abstract thinking. They adhere to accidental examples, to literal formulations, instead of grasping the real point, the meaning, the intention of what has been said.

Sancho Panza in Cervantes' novel *Don Quixote* illustrates this type of holding to the letter in answering Don Quixote's admonitions concerning his governship of the island. Don Quixote says that Sancho should not lose sight of "the consideration of your having been a swineherd in your own country,..." to which Sancho answers: "true when I was a boy I kept swine, later when I grew towards man I looked after geese and not after hogs."[1] Instead of grasping the spirit of Don Quixote's words, namely that he should not forget, as governor, the modest circumstances of his youth, Sancho considers only the kind of animal he watched over—an item having no importance whatever for the "spirit" of the admonition.

This kind of abiding by the letter can be traced back to intellectual insufficiency. It has a naïve and ludicrous character. It is altogether different from pharisaic adherence to the letter.

When practiced with regard to moral commandments and prescriptions, however, this holding to the letter may lay bare a kind of obstinacy and spiritual laziness. One does not take the trouble to penetrate to the spirit. One considers oneself to be especially obedient and exact by mechanically applying a rule, a moral prescription, or a piece of advice without making use of one's intelligence. In short, it is the rule applied with blindfold eyes.

In the worst of cases, this way of mechanically obeying advice or a command may even be motivated by the intent of carrying out an unwelcome order to the point of absurdity, or at least by the desire to withdraw from any sense of personal responsibility of one's own. Up to this point, "letter"

---

[1] *Don Quixote,* Volume II, Chapter 42.

always refers to accidental details, while "spirit" to the true meaning of a proposition.

Another type of "abiding by the letter" is to be found in the morally timorous man.[2] He stands by the letter because it is the letter alone that suffices to set his conscience at peace. If departing from the letter of a commandment were still in conformity with the spirit, he would nevertheless abide by the letter. Even if the spirit of a moral precept should, in an extraordinary situation, require him to depart from the letter, he would never take the risk of doing so.

This type of fixation on the letter is not restricted to the timorous man, as we saw in the previous chapter. It may also be motivated by a kind of rigoristic pedantry. It does not have the character of enmity against the spirit, but it results rather from a lack of freedom of spirit. One insists on a fulfillment of the letter. Anything that departs from the letter, even if such departure were truly consistent with the spirit, is rejected as insufficient. This "abiding by the letter" is accomplished with the consciousness of being morally stricter than others. The pedantic rigorist believes himself to be more conscientious, and he suspects laxism in every failure to correspond to the letter (even when departing from the letter is in accordance with the spirit). To refer to the spirit instead of the letter is already something to be suspicious of in his eyes, an attempt to elude the commandments. In other words, for him the spirit is *always* so linked to the letter that any deviation from the letter necessarily implies a betrayal of the spirit. According to him, one fulfills the commandment in a fully conscientious way and takes the commandment seriously only by holding strictly to the letter.

It is this type of "abiding by the letter" that is the very opposite of freedom of spirit. In these cases, "letter" may refer to the nonessential formulation as well as to the

[2] Cf. Chapter II, p. 32 ff.

isolation of a precept, while "spirit" may refer to the true meaning of a precept or to the spirit of morality as such.

A fourth type of conflict between letter and spirit can be found in the case of the typical bureaucrat. For this type, whom we have mentioned in another chapter, only juridically formulated things count, or at least only that which is subject to juridical categories. The commandment to love God and our neighbor seems to him nebulous and vague. "Thou shalt not kill," he will accept as precise and realistic. He will tend to place the juridical sphere above the moral and will try to reduce all moral obligations to juridical ones.[3] That part of morality that withstands this attempt is not acknowledged by him, or it is considered as more or less romantic. He abides by the letter because the letter alone is real for him. In this case again, "letter" may refer to the details of formulation as well as to the isolated commandment, while "spirit" may refer to the true meaning as well as to the spirit of morality as such.

A fifth case of abiding by the letter is to be found in the mediocre man, who contents himself with the letter of a commandment and does not grasp the invitation to do more than the commandment literally requires. He is the man who says, "I am a good Catholic; I fulfill my Easter Duty every year. The Church requires only that we go to confession and communion on Easter. Why should I do more?" To abide by the letter here means contenting oneself with the minimum of what is strictly required in its literal formulation, instead of grasping the invitation to transcend this minimum. Instead of seeing that the letter is here meant as a mere minimum, one interprets it as embracing the totality of what is desirable, and as expressing everything that the spirit of the commandment encourages. This kind of adherence to the letter does not have a hypocritical character, nor does it involve any enmity against the spirit, leaving no

[3] Cf. Chapter V, "Freedom of Spirit."

room for it; but it is the specific mark of moral mediocrity in its different forms, whether a naïve mediocrity or a self-righteous mediocre correctness. In this case "letter" means the isolated commandment as opposed to the spirit out of which this commandment flows.

We now come to the last type of "abiding by the letter," which is typical of pharisaism. We find it exemplified in the Gospel passage in which the Pharisees blame our Lord because he cured a sick man on the Sabbath. The spirit of the third commandment forbids work on a day that should be a day of contemplation and leisure in the highest sense of these terms. But the fact that this day belongs to God in a specific manner in no way means that it excludes charitable actions, especially the help that an emergency demands. To interpret the Sabbath commandment in the sense of excluding every activity, to miss the radical difference between working and acts of charity—not to speak of a miraculous healing—is a specific evasion of the spirit in holding to the letter.

Here a commandment is misinterpreted and isolated. It is upheld against the spirit of morality and God's will. The specific hypocrisy of this attitude consists in disobedience carried out in the name of obedience. Here both meanings of letter and spirit are clearly involved. But the specific mark here is that "abiding by the letter" is voluntarily and purposely accomplished. It springs from the hypocritical desire to evade the spirit while simultaneously conserving the consciousness of being morally correct.

It is especially in judging other persons that one abides by the letter. "Abiding by the letter" assumes then the character of an odious rigidity and a means for the pharisee's merciless sentence. It becomes an instrument of pseudo justice. It betrays the desire to condemn other persons and one's satisfaction when one succeeds in doing so. It is part of the general desubstantialization of morality that is so typical of pharisaism.

In enumerating the different cases of "abiding by the letter" we can clearly detect two basic attitudes:

First, one follows the letter while ignoring the spirit. "Abiding by the letter" here means to be contented with a minimum of moral effort. Such is the case of the previously mentioned mediocre, correct man.

In the other basic attitude, "abiding by the letter" means that for the sake of moral safety one never wants to depart from the letter. One is content only when, in addition to the spirit, the letter is observed. Such is the case of the morally timorous man.

In the former case, the letter is substituted for the spirit. In the latter case, the letter is made the indispensable condition and guarantee of fulfilling the spirit and thus, as it were, imprisons the spirit. This distinction, which we mentioned already in the foregoing chapter when discussing the timorous type, is here more emphatically restated because it is of the utmost importance in answering the questions of when and where a distinction between letter and spirit can be made in the field of moral commandments, or of when and where this distinction can be applied. We shall see later on that whereas in many cases it is impossible to fulfill the spirit in departing from the letter, to observe the letter without fulfilling the spirit is always possible.

When dealing with certain commandments we shall see that "abiding by the letter" is neither pedantry nor timorousness. For although it may not yet be the totality of what is morally required, it is morally obligatory.

We have already mentioned that it is always possible to elude the spirit though one fulfills the letter. It is possible with respect to all moral commandments, as well as to positive commandments, and in all three meanings of letter and spirit.[4] Someone may abstain from committing adultery in

---

[4] There are, however, commandments that exclude *ab ovo* any discrepancy of letter and spirit. This is the case with respect to the fundamental commandments of Christ: the love of God and the love of neighbor. Here the commandments refer to attitudes and not to actions; thus, on the one hand,

the literal sense, while yet committing it, as it were, spiritually. Or to take another case, the Pharisees, in inciting the people of Israel and Pilate to crucify Christ, did not violate the letter of the commandment, "Thou shalt not kill," but they clearly violated the spirit of the commandment.

The same applies to positive commandments. Someone may attend Mass on Sunday, thereby fulfilling the letter of the commandment. But if he reads a newspaper during Mass he clearly violates the spirit of this same commandment.

The same is true if we take "letter" in the sense of action and "spirit" in the sense of the motive underlying this action. If someone approaches moral commandments as if they were only conventional rules of conduct, submitting to them in the same spirit and with the same motives that lead him to wear fashionable clothes, he eludes the spirit, though he fulfills the letter. He evades the spirit by failing to co-operate subjectively, that is, by failing to respond to the values that they already include the *finis operantis*; on the other hand, the very nature of these attitudes implies many actions and excludes many others. These commandments also exclude all those actions that are immoral already by the *finis operis*. These prescribed attitudes are not vague, but are utterly concrete and precise. The love of God implies obedience to all His commandments: "If anyone loves me, he will keep my word."

In the last chapter of this work we shall see how the structure of these two commandments "upon which dependeth all the laws and the prophets" reveals in a specific way the nature of Christian morality. Here we want to stress that when dealing with these two commandments we cannot even fulfill the letter without fulfilling the spirit—the formulation is such that letter and spirit coincide. It is the unique case in which any antagonism whatever between letter and spirit is excluded.

The only discrepancy that can possibly be found here is the one between the appearance of charity and true charity; but it would be clearly a very artificial and inadequate terminology to call merely apparent signs of charity, "letter," and true charity, "spirit." The antithesis of a mere verbal charity and true charity is clearly of another type than the one of letter and spirit.

The two commandments of Christ, however, not only include other commandments such as the Decalogue, thereby making it impossible to keep the former while disregarding the latter; they also do not substitute for them in the sense of making the formulation of other moral commandments superfluous, for these other commandments indicate precisely what is implied by the love of God.

are the very reason of the commandments. He is not motivated by these values, and still less is he motivated by obedience to God. He thus remains in a merely exterior, conventional contact with these commandments.[5]

The same applies to positive commandments. Someone who goes to church only because he wants to make a good impression on his employer, in order to be promoted, but lacks faith and the spirit of obedience to the Church, fulfills the letter but evades the spirit.

A fulfillment of the letter while avoiding the spirit is also possible if we take "letter" in the sense of isolated commandments and "spirit" in the sense of the spirit of morality as such, that is, the spirit out of which these commandments flow. Thus someone may fulfill the commandment of going to church on Sunday but only by leaving a helpless, sick relative who should be taken care of. It is also possible with respect to moral commandments: we may fail to love God and our neighbor though we abstain from adultery, homicide, theft, and sacrilegious acts.[6]

As soon as we ask when can the spirit be fulfilled though departing from the letter, a completely different picture is offered to us. First, we must say this, that if we take "letter" in the sense of the literal formulation of a commandment and "spirit" in the sense of the intention and meaning of the commandment, it is never possible to fulfill the spirit without fulfilling the letter when moral commandments including an absolute veto are in question. For example, an absolute veto is found in the moral commandments: "Thou shalt not commit adultery," "Thou shalt not curse," or "Thou shalt not sacrifice to idols or deny God." Here it is absolutely impossible to claim that someone could ever depart from the letter without violating the spirit, that is, without sinning.

---

[5] Clearly, we do not intend to say that this case of fulfilling the letter and evading the spirit constitutes a sin. It is merely the absence of a moral value.

[6] Eluding the spirit in the sense of "spirit of morality," with respect to moral commandments is mostly combined with the absence of adequate motives.

It makes no sense to say that although someone committed adultery in the literal sense of the word he remains true to the spirit of the commandment—if we take "spirit" in the sense of the meaning and intention of the commandment. The formulation here is such that "spirit" necessarily includes the letter, so that the possibility of any departure from the letter without violating the spirit is excluded regardless of the circumstances.

The same applies to positive commandments. It is impossible to say, "I do not go to Mass on Sunday, but nevertheless I fulfill the spirit of this commandment." [7] Here the formulation is such that a distinction between letter and spirit in the sense of unessential and essential cannot be made. It is impossible to fulfill the spirit in departing from the letter, since the letter is the true and strict formulation of the spirit. Though one can fail to fulfill the spirit in fulfilling the letter, as we saw before, here one never can fulfill the spirit without fulfilling the letter.

Only in the field of moral advice, casuistic applications, or rules of prudence, can we deviate from the letter that is, if we always take "letter" in the sense of nonessential versus essential.

If the formulation is such that nonessential details are included, departing from the letter insofar as those details are concerned is clearly possible without violating the spirit. In these cases it might even be imperative to depart from the letter in order to remain true to the spirit.

The same applies if we take "letter" as being the action and "spirit" as the required value response or the true motives on account of which an evil action is omitted. When moral commandments with an absolute veto are in question, it is impossible to depart from the letter without sinning. When morally relevant goods, which are contradicted, injured, or destroyed, are such that an action in relation to them is morally bad and sinful independently of the underlying motives, the spirit can never compensate for the moral

[7] We here take for granted that there is no valid excuse.

evil of the action itself. The action is morally bad in any case and is an offense against God. It is always and everywhere imperative to abstain from this type of action. It is always strictly obligatory to fulfill the letter in this sense.[8]

In cases in which the moral disvalue of an action presupposes a specific intention and motive underlying this action, it may be possible to depart from the letter without violating the commandments. There are many actions that may have an opposite moral significance according to the motive underlying them. If someone mutilates an enemy by cutting off his arm, it is a horrible crime. If the surgeon does the same in order to save a patient's life, it is not only morally justified, but even morally good. If a father makes his child suffer by punishing him out of real love, because of a true interest in the child's welfare, his action is morally good and even under certain circumstances obligatory. But if someone makes a child suffer in the same way because of sadistic tendencies, the action is morally despicable. In all these cases a discrepancy of letter and spirit could occur, but clearly no moral commandment refers merely to these actions without including a reference to the motive in the formulation of the commandment. Commandments, insofar as they refer to actions that receive their moral significance only through a specific intention and through specific motives, include in their formulation a reference to the nature of the intention.

As far as moral commandments including an absolute veto are concerned, it is also impossible to depart from the letter without violating the spirit, in the sense of the "spirit of morality." It is impossible to commit adultery or fornication

[8] There are, however, moral commandments in which a difference between letter and spirit can be made in a certain sense. "Thou shalt not kill" is an absolute veto, and no intention, friendly as it may be, would allow us to arrogate to ourselves the right to decide on the life of a human being. Even euthanasia committed out of compassion remains a terrible sin. However, to kill in self-defense when assailed by an aggressor is morally allowed. Some radical pacifists who consider every killing as included in the commandment "Thou shalt not kill" would be examples of abiding by the letter. The man killing an aggressor in legitimate self-defense departs from the letter without violating the spirit.

and to remain true to the spirit of morality. Never and nowhere could these actions be morally unobjectionable. This type of discrepancy is only possible insofar as commandments are at stake that can be overruled by another moral obligation. We are, for instance, morally obliged to keep a promise, granted that the content is morally unobjectionable. But if having promised to do a job at a certain time, or to visit someone, we suddenly come upon a person whose life is in danger, or if any great emergency occurs, we have to break our promise in order to lend our assistance. Here it would be morally wrong to "abide by the letter," for the very spirit makes it imperative for us to abstain from fulfilling this commandment. Hence in this case, it is not only allowed but even morally obligatory to depart from the letter.

The same applies to positive commandments. If we are facing the alternative either of going to Mass or of endangering a sick relative in leaving him alone, we have to depart from the letter (here, of the positive commandment), following the spirit of morality, which imposes on us the obligation to remain with our sick relative.

The foregoing analysis has shown that when confronted with moral commandments including an absolute veto, it is in no circumstance possible to depart from the letter without violating the spirit, that is, without sinning. This applies to all three possible meanings of "spirit" and "letter."

Thus it is a great error of circumstance ethics to view unshakable obedience to the fundamental moral commandments including an absolute veto as merely a narrow "abiding by the letter." In interpreting the conduct of the moral man who in any circumstance respects the absolute veto of moral commandments as being the narrowness of the pedantic bureaucrat or of the self-righteous man, the adherents of circumstance ethics try to discredit the validity of true moral commandments and precisely disregard the spirit of morality.

It is here that one of the main errors of circumstance ethics comes to the fore. Its champions want to oust all general moral commandments, emphasizing that every moral decision is unique. We shall see later on [9] the impossibility of expelling general moral principles. Here we want to stress that all the arguments in favor of the "spirit" and against the "letter" and all the criticism of mediocrity prove absolutely nothing against the absolute validity of the general moral principles because their absolute veto excludes any possibility of ever departing from the letter.

The exponents of circumstance ethics deal with all moral commandments as if they received their moral significance only through a certain intention, and ignore the fact that certain actions are morally illegitimate and sinful, whatever the intention may be.

[9] Cf. Chapter X, "Basic Errors of Circumstance Ethics."

Chapter V

# FREEDOM OF SPIRIT

There is a certain antagonism between spirit and letter, in an analogous sense, which perhaps is behind the attempt of circumstance ethics to substitute the voice of conscience alone for general principles and moral commandments. Circumstance ethics includes a protest against the moral bureaucrat, and to a certain extent against the morally timorous man. It contrasts their desire to find safety in juridically formulated moral obligations with the "personal risk" of the man who relies on his conscience alone.

In order to understand the problem that lies beneath this trend, we must touch upon certain differences that we find in the realm of moral obligations. Certain moral obligations are accessible to juridical terms; they are connected with juridical liabilities. Such, for instance, is the obligation to meet the terms of a contract, or to return borrowed money to the lender. Other moral obligations are not accessible to juridical terms and are not connected with legal liabilities, for example, the obligation to help a person in a great emergency.[1] Such an obligation is clearly not connected with anything pertaining to the juridical sphere.

We shall call the first type of moral obligation "formal" and the second type "material." All moral obligations that are immediately and exclusively rooted in morally relevant values are "material" in our terminology. Such is the obligation to love and adore God, Infinite Goodness Itself. Such is the obligation to love our neighbor, created to the image

[1] We take it for granted that the fact that help can be given without grave risk to oneself makes it obligatory.

and likeness of God. Such is the obligation to be pure, by giving the due response to the mystery of the sphere of sex. Such is the obligation to respect truth and to abstain from lying. Such, too, are the obligations to be humble and to be just. Most moral commandments, in fact, represent this type of obligation.

Moral obligations that have, more or less, a connection with juridical bonds and imply the presence of such bonds are "formal" in our terminology. Such is the moral obligation to keep a promise, to accomplish what I have agreed to do by contract, or to fulfill the duties required by a function that I have freely assumed or that has been imposed on me by the course of events.

It would exceed our present purpose to broach the problem of the relation between the moral and the juridical spheres.[2] We must restrict ourselves by dealing with this problem only to the extent that is necessary in order to understand certain sources of the thesis of circumstance ethics and to elaborate certain features of Christian morality.

We have mentioned several times that there exists a widespread tendency to adapt morality to the juridical sphere and attempt to apply juridical categories to it. A further analysis now of the difference in the realm of moral obligation to which we have so far adverted, will also serve to throw light on this tendency.

We have to realize first that legal bonds are objective and

---

[2] The relation between the sphere of juridical entities (including all types of rights and contracts) and the moral sphere is eminently a philosophical problem. Its analysis presupposes an ontology of the juridical sphere, an inquiry into the strange character of these entities and their immanent a priori laws.

This sphere has often been overlooked in its specific character. It has either been declared to be a mere conventional fiction or it has been more or less identified with the moral sphere. With regard to the latter position, one can say that while it has many essential relations to the moral sphere, it still has its own "logos." Hence, to do justice to the true relation between the moral and the juridical spheres, one would have to analyze the nature of the juridical sphere as something having its own specific character.

in no way mere conventions or fictions.³ The act of making a promise clearly creates a real bond between me and the person to whom I promise something. I am free to bring it into existence, but once it is there it is no longer in my power to withdraw it. Only when I fulfill my promise will this bond vanish. This bond has the character of being a "liability" on my part and of being a right or title on the part of the one to whom I have made a promise. Another social act endowed with creative power is the contract, an act in which two persons co-operate to give birth to a legal entity that binds them.⁴

What matters in our context is to understand that the legal bond issuing from certain social acts, such as that of promising, also implies a moral obligation. I am morally obliged to keep my promises if their content is not immoral or physically impossible of fulfillment. I am obliged to accomplish duties that I have formally and voluntarily accepted, for instance, to accomplish a certain work, or to take care of a child.

The formal moral obligation has an apparent advantage over the material one with respect to intelligibility.

For many persons, the obligation to pay back borrowed money or to meet a bill seems more intelligible than the obligation of gratitude, for example, the obligation to help a person in need who has done much for us in former times. Again, they will consider the obligation of gratitude to be relatively more intelligible than one of pure charity, for example, the obligation to help an unknown man in great need.

To the extent that they can find a basis for an obligation without taking morally relevant values into account, these

---

³ Cf. Adolph Reinach, *Apriori in bürgerlichen Recht, Gesammelte Schriften* (Halle: M. Niemeyer).

Cf. also D. von Hildebrand, *"Die rechtliche und sittliche Sphaere in ihrem Eigenwert und in ihrem Zusammenhang," Menschheit am Scheideweg*, pp. 86–107.

⁴ We could add several other examples, such as the vote of a legislative assembly, which gives birth to a law.

people erroneously consider themselves to be on firmer ground. For they believe they are then dealing with something more intelligible. The more "formal" the obligation is, in the sense already given to this term, the more readily will they admit that it is a moral obligation. To help a relative seems obligatory. He has a right, after all, to claim it. To help an unknown person, where no tangible bond is to be found that could in any way be translated into juridical terms, seems quite unintelligible.

The prototype of a formal moral obligation is the one referring to the fulfillment of a contract or a promise. Here the connection with juridical liability is especially clear, and the most radical moral bureaucrat will even be tempted to confuse altogether the moral obligation with the legal liability.[5]

But this temptation is not restricted to the bureaucrat. For those who consider that proofs and arguments yield a higher degree of intelligibility than self-evidence are also likely to regard a formal moral obligation as having a higher kind of intelligibility than the material moral obligation. They will consequently tend to reduce all moral obligations to formal ones, that is, to rights on the part of God or on the part of our neighbor, and so on. This is precisely what we mean by the erroneous interpretation of morality in juridical terms that we have so often mentioned.

Actually, however, formal moral obligations are in no way more intelligible than material ones. Indeed it is rather the material obligations, and not the formal ones, that disclose the true nature of morality and the moral sphere in a more typical way. They call for a focusing on the very essence of morality and for an independent understanding of the spirit of morality, of its specific "inner logos," without recourse to data borrowed from the sphere of rights. To understand the

---

[5] The nature of the connection between formal moral obligations and juridical bonds will be analyzed in a later publication. There it will be shown that formal obligations are also ultimately rooted in values, although more indirectly than material obligations.

relation between the morally relevant values and God, to find in them God's will and spirit, means to enter in a much more authentic way into the very "marrow" of morality. The formal obligations are thus only seemingly more intelligible, owing to the fact that here one is able to reach an intelligibility without piercing through to the soul of morality, that is, without realizing the role that values play. It is tantamount to finding the "letter" more intelligible than the "spirit."

Furthermore, it is impossible to interpret the most fundamental moral obligations, that is, material obligations, as formal, as based on rights or legal bonds. To do so would be to violate their very nature, and thus to conceal their true intelligibility.[6]

Yet we must clearly distinguish between those who, because of the apparent superior intelligibility of formal obligation, try to find an analogous explanation for all moral commandments, and the type of man whom we have called a moral bureaucrat. The former will recognize all moral obligations, material as well as formal, but—for the sake of an assumed higher intelligibility—they will try, from a theoretical point of view, to interpret all moral obligations in terms of formal obligations. The moral bureaucrat, on the contrary, is more or less blind to material obligations. He will grasp only the obligation that has by its very nature a formal character. It is this mentality that is our specific topic here.

The distinction between formal and material moral obligation must not be confused with several others that play a great role in the realm of morality.

Our distinction does not refer to the difference between an obligation rooted in justice and one rooted in charity, because, though justice also embraces formal moral obligations, it is in no way restricted to these obligations. If someone agrees to work for me for a given salary, the moral obligation connected here with a juridical liability requires that

[6] To say that irreverence against God is evil because God has a "right" to be treated reverently is obviously missing the point.

I fulfill my contract. Yet it may well be that objectively the salary is inadequate even though the employee has agreed to it. In this case I may fulfill the formal moral obligation resulting from the contract, but at the same time I act unjustly. Thus justice reaches much further than the fulfillment of formal obligations. Though the commandments of charity may be the most typical examples of the nonjuridical part of morality, it would be quite wrong to identify the commandments of justice with the realm of formal moral obligations.

Again we must beware of confusing the distinction between formal and material moral obligations with the distinction between moral obligations and moral calls that are not obligatory. There are nonobligatory actions and attitudes that are obviously morally praiseworthy and endowed with high moral values. For instance, to save the life of another person by risking one's own is eminently good morally, but it is not obligatory. The difference between the obligatory and the nonobligatory entails a fundamental ethical problem that will be discussed in detail in later publications. But the distinction we are concerned with is to be found within the realm of moral obligations. It is of paramount importance to understand that the formal character of the obligations that go hand in hand with juridical liabilities must be clearly distinguished from the character of obligation as such. For it is obligation that precisely is proper to the commandments rooted in morally relevant values and ultimately in God's nature, in other words, in material obligations.

Our distinction between two types of moral obligation must likewise not be reduced to the difference between obedience and love. Someone might say that the realm of obedience is strict, tangible, and able to be expressed in clear-cut formulas, whereas the realm of charity, on the contrary, calls for a more intuitive and spontaneous understanding, and the appeals made by love are more resistant to juridical formulation and have to be "felt." He may conclude from this that it is precisely the difference between the two realms of obedience and love that is at the bottom of the distinction between formal and material moral obligations. But this is not the case. We have to fulfill both types of moral obligations. Both by their obligatory character call for obedience.

Nevertheless, although the differences between justice and charity, between the obligatory and the nonobligatory moral calls, and between obedience and love must all be clearly distinguished from the difference between formal and material moral obligations, there is some analogy between them. The man who has the tendency to restrict morality to formal moral obligations will more easily understand a commandment imposed by justice than one commanded by charity. He will also be disposed to ignore everything that is not obligatory. To such a mentality obligations alone will be regarded as serious. Moral calls that are not obligatory will appear to him as unsubstantial and nebulous. Finally he will have the tendency to recognize in morality only obedience. Love will be something extramoral for him. He will claim that anything that is not accessible to juridical categories is devoid of intelligibility. He will locate it somewhere in the sphere of indefinite and fluctuating feelings.

Thus we can see that the difference between formal and material moral obligations must be clearly distinguished from these other differences just enumerated in the realm of morality, while, on the other hand, certain analogies between them must be recognized. These analogies are primarily reflected in the bureaucratic mentality. The radical bureaucrat will admit only moral obligations rooted in legal liabilities. The less radical bureaucrat will admit other obligations also, but only to the extent that they have some analogy with formal obligations.

Our distinction between formal and material obligations comes very close to the classical distinction between positive and moral commandments. Yet it is not identical with it. Positive commandments, it is true, share with formal obligations the element of an apparent superior intelligibility. Not only positive commandments have this formal character, however, for clearly the obligation to keep one's promise is not a positive commandment. Moreover, the positive commandments of God and of Holy Church on the other hand, have a sacred dignity that definitely surpasses what we have called the formal obligations. The infinitely holy will of God confers on the content of what is commanded a sublime value. Certainly, this value is superimposed, in contradistinction to the content of moral commandments, which reflect God's nature in their very being. But a divine positive commandment, because of the Absolute Person who imposes it, also embodies a high morally relevant value. And this applies analogously to the commandments of Holy Church. The obedience to both always has the character of a value response, and the moral obligation in question is never a purely formal one.[7]

Thus, in spite of a certain affinity, the difference between formal and material moral obligations does not coincide with the one between moral and positive commandments.

As we have seen, the moral bureaucrat feels that he is morally obligated primarily when prescriptions with a formal and more or less juridical character are in question. To keep a contract will weigh more heavily on the bureaucrat's conscience than to help an unknown person in an emergency. To betray a friend will seem to the moral bureaucrat less serious than to betray a legal partner. To fulfill professional duties seems to him more important than to console a man in deep distress.

Furthermore, people like the moral bureaucrat will see no moral obligation whatever in a situation that does not fit into any formulated general moral commandment. They will not be able to understand the moral invitation and still less the obligation issuing from morally relevant values in an unforeseen situation.

The Parable of the Good Samaritan is the basic example of this incapacity. The priest and the Levite both pass by

[7] Cf. D. von Hildebrand, *"Das Wesen der echten Autorität,"* *Menschheit am Scheideweg* (Regensburg: Habbel, 1954), pp. 341–407.

and do not minister to the man in distress because no formal moral obligation compels them to do so. They would probably have taken care of the wounded man had he been a brother or a relative, or if he had been someone formally entrusted to their care. But the call issuing here from this man's grave situation, his ordeal, on the one hand, and the value of a human being on the other, is not grasped.

The moral bureaucrat's standard word is, "That is no business of mine." He will be conscious of his duty to pay back money to a rich man from whom he borrowed it. But he will not understand the moral call of justice to pay an employee adequately. The fact that the latter has agreed to work for him at a stipulated salary is enough to satisfy his conscience. Still less will he understand the call of charity to help a poor man who has no *juridical* claim whatever on him.

The timorous man, on the contrary, is not blind to material obligations. But because of his timorousness, he feels he is on firmer ground and that his conscience is more protected when he can rely on formal obligations. Formal obligations weigh on his conscience to such an extent that, in case they conflict with a material obligation, he never will decide in favor of the latter. The formal obligation assumes the character of a strait jacket for him and prevents him from following the call of God in such a situation. He may worry about his lack of courage, which prevents him from following an urgent call of charity, but formal obligations have such a hold on his conscience that he is unable to withstand their pressure. Yet so long as no formal obligation is at stake he may be open to all obligations that justice and charity impose.

The bohemian, on the contrary, will ignore all formal obligations. He will not feel compelled, for example, to pay back the money he borrowed from a rich man.

Christian freedom of spirit implies that no extramoral factor be permitted to intervene as an obstacle to one's conforming to the superior moral obligation. It is as remote from the bureaucrat's attachment to formal obligation as it is from the bohemian's aversion to formal obligation.

In Christian morality the commandments of charity have, as such, precedence over merely formal obligations. But this does not mean that formal commandments lack full validity in Christian morality. Far from being invalidated, they assume even a greater import. But the commandments resulting in a more immediate way from charity are still superior and must be given precedence in case of conflict.[8]

The Parable of the Good Samaritan illustrates the emphasis placed on the obligation of charity in the Gospel. The Samaritan not only has no formal obligation whatever toward the wounded man, but the wounded man is not even one of his own people. He is a Jew, with whom the Samaritans would have no dealings. And that it is *he* precisely who is offered as an example of who one's neighbor is throws into relief, through this new conception of the notion of neighbor, the primacy of the call of charity over all formal obligations.[9]

---

[8] Sometimes we find the attempt to create an antithesis between Christian charity and the juridical sphere. The "loving Church" is opposed to the "Church of rights," or the "Johanine Church" to the "Petrine," patently in order to claim that the Church of love is the true, pneumatic one. This is a grave and disastrous error. We hope to show in this book how far Christian morality is from disrespecting the realm of juridical entities and from invalidating what we have termed formal obligations. The priority of charity, far from invalidating the sphere of formal obligations, pervades it, giving it a new, sublime aspect. The Church of love and the Church of rights are two aspects of one and the same Church. The one who really understands the nature of the juridical structure proper to the Church and its difference from a mere temporal right, will discover in this structure the breath of divine law and divine charity.

[9] The last visit of St. Benedict to his sister St. Scholastica illustrates the precedence of charity in Christian morality.

"When darkness was setting in, they took their meal together and continued their conversation at table until it was quite late. Then the holy nun said to him: 'Please do not leave me tonight, brother. Let us keep on talking about the joys of heaven till morning.' 'What are you saying, sister?' he replied. 'You know I cannot stay away from the monastery.'

"The sky was so clear at the time, there was not a cloud in sight. At her brother's refusal Scholastica folded her hands on the table and rested her head upon them in earnest prayer. When she looked up again, there was a sudden burst of lightning and thunder accompanied by such a down-pour that Benedict and his companions were unable to set foot outside the door....

"Realizing that he could not return to the abbey in this terrible storm,

In order to understand more completely the moral bureaucrat's mentality, as well as how true freedom of spirit displays itself in the case of a conflict between formal and material obligations, we must take other factors into consideration. It is that between the weight of an obligation and the good to which a liability refers there exists a close connection. The content of what has to be fulfilled has a decisive bearing on the nature of both the social act and the moral obligation created by it. For example, a promise to go to a dance with someone obviously has not the weight and impact of a promise to marry someone.

It is easy to see that, although the social act, as such, creates the liability, the content of what is promised has a decisive bearing on the nature of the moral obligation connected with that liability. Not only do the weight and impact of the act of promising vary according to its object but, also the moral obligation to keep the promise varies in its character. The higher the content of a promise or a contract ranks, the more the moral obligation to keep them increases. Thus the formal obligation does not stand by itself but generally implies a material obligation as well.[10]

In case of conflicting calls, let us say, on the one hand, a duty connected with a liability, for example, a professional

---

Benedict complained bitterly. 'God forgive you, sister!' he said. 'What have you done?'

"Scholastica simply answered, 'When I appealed to you, you would not listen to me. So I turned to my God and He heard my prayer. Leave now if you can. Leave me here and go back to your monastery.'

"This, of course, he could not do. He had no choice now but to stay, in spite of his unwillingness. They spent the entire night together and both of them derived great profit from the holy thoughts they exchanged about the interior life." Taken from St. Gregory the Great's *Life and Miracles of St. Benedict,* Newly Translated by Odo J. Zimmermann, O.S.B., and Benedict R. Avery, O.S.B., pp. 67-69.

The Liturgy comments upon this event with the words: "*Dominum rogavit, et ab eo plus potuit, quia plus amavit*" (She made a request of the Lord, and it carried more weight because she loved more). (Magnificat, Antiphon of the Feast of St. Scholastica.)

[10] It is an obvious fact, of course, that the immoral content of a promise would dissolve any moral obligation.

duty, and on the other, the call of a morally relevant value, for example, an emergency in which another person finds himself, the character of the good to which the liability refers clearly plays a great role. For it may be not only that a formal obligation stands against a material one, but that material obligations are interwoven with formal ones. For example, one should undoubtedly break a promise to play bridge if suddenly another person needs him at that very time for a fairly important reason. If, on the contrary, instead of a promise to play bridge, there is in question a promise to deliver an important lecture, or a contract that binds one to complete a work by a certain date, a more serious material moral obligation would have to press its claim upon one to compel him to break the bond created by the promise or by the contract.

But apart from this enhancing of formal obligation through the importance of its content—which as we have seen, adds to it a material obligation—there is also a gradation to be found on the basis of the very character of a "binding" act that is not determined by the content, though it is not without relation to it. We are referring to the degree of solemnity with which a promise or a contract is entered into. We can either merely promise something, or we can solemnly give a promise. We can give to the promise a more weighty character by having witnesses to it. We can even elevate it to an extraordinary degree of solemnity by invoking God as witness, by promising with an oath or in the name of God.

This also manifestly has a great bearing on the nature of the moral obligation to keep a promise.[11] However, the degree of weight that a promise may assume by the name in which it is given has also a relation to morally relevant values,

---

[11] The weight of such a promise or of such a contract, though in this case not resulting from the content, but from the emphasis laid on the promise and the name in which it is given, has nevertheless a relation to the content. A certain emphasis requires an important content in order to be serious or to avoid becoming an object of ridicule.

though the influence of morally relevant values stemming from this source is more indirect than the one resulting from the nature of the content. The influence brought to bear on the nature of a promise by the invocation of God clearly stems from the absolute value of the name of God.

One of the principal factors increasing the weight of a moral obligation to keep a promise is the significance of the promised content for the person to whom the promise is made.

Two kinds of significance must here be distinguished. First, we must ask what it *objectively* means to him. Is it a high objective good for him, something having a bearing on his moral good? Is it something that would be a great source of happiness to him if he were able to appreciate it? Is it perhaps an elementary good indispensable for his very existence? It must be emphasized that as soon as a promise refers to such matters as these, keeping the promise is no longer a purely formal obligation, but also a commandment of charity. Here the two obligations flow together. My duty to help the person in question is not only the call of charity that would exist independently of any promise, and would accrue only to the purely formal obligation; but it is an obligation of charity to be faithful to a promise concerning such a high objective good for him. The fact that I have committed myself to take care of such a good, that the other person is counting on me, makes the fulfillment of the promise a material as well as a formal obligation. Even though the other person is not particularly concerned about my fulfillment of the promise, blind perhaps to the true objective good for him at stake, there would still be present an obligation of charity in addition to the formal obligation. Once I have placed myself in a responsible relation to matters concerning another person's welfare, failure to keep my promise would be immoral, not only because a formal moral obligation is not being fulfilled, but also because of a definite lack of charity and a lack of interest in his welfare on my part.

We now come to the second kind of significance. Even if the content of a promise is not a high objective good for another person, the role that it plays for him subjectively may make it an obligation of charity for me to keep my promise. The person with whom we promise to play bridge may have an inferiority complex, for example, and failure to keep our promise to him may have disastrous psychological consequences for him. The content of a promise may be unimportant. But psychological circumstances can give to its fulfillment a completely different moral import. Certainly, if morally illegitimate motives are in question, such a material obligation will not be added to the purely formal one. The fact that another person is hypersensitive, that because of his pride he will be deeply offended if I do not keep my promise, is of no moral importance. So long as the bad psychological effects on the person with whom I promised to play bridge are the consequences of morally illegitimate attitudes, of his presumptuousness, pride, arrogance, or childish passion to play cards, only a formal obligation to keep the promise is present and no material obligation of charity.

Only weakness, a special vulnerability, psychological disposition not brought on directly by vice, but resulting from former sufferings, disillusionments, or trials, may add a material obligation of charity to the formal one to keep a promise. A new moral call to keep our promise is emphatically present if the dispositions on the part of the other person are such that such a minor disappointment may endanger him morally.

The fact that another person counts on my fulfillment of a promise, that he may deeply suffer by my disappointing him, and especially that it may have bad consequences for his soul if I do not keep my word, makes the keeping of a promise an obligation of charity, independently of the objective rank of the content of the promise.

The perversion of the moral bureaucrat manifests itself again in this connection. He will, in all cases of legal liability, take into account only the formal obligation. He will feel himself compelled to fulfill a promise to help someone in an emergency primarily because of the purely formal obligation. The call of charity interwoven in this promise will not weigh on his conscience. He will ignore the gradations that exist in the realm of formal obligation. He will take the fulfillment of every promise with equal seriousness, regardless of its content. And in cases in which a formal obligation is in conflict with a material obligation, it is to the formal one that he will defer.

Even formal obligations themselves, however, are taken more seriously by the true Christian than by the moral bureaucrat. Because his life is consciously lived in God's sight, formal obligations assume a solemnity and seriousness that is beyond the bureaucrat's comprehension. The basic attitude of *religio*—the consciousness of being only a steward, one's awareness of the account he must render to God—gives to every task assumed and to every formal obligation a new value and weight. But for the very same reasons that induce the true Christian to take the formal moral obligations more seriously, he will also fully grasp the material obligations that are interwoven with formal obligations. Moreover, he will give the call of charity preference. Failure to keep a promise will weigh heavily on his conscience more because of the lack of charity connected with it, than because of the lack of reliability it implies.

In cases of conflict between material and formal obligations, formal obligations will never act as a strait jacket to hinder the true Christian from conforming to the morally superior call and from assigning to charity the last word.

Neither the psychological weight that something assumes because of habit, nor one's aversion to full responsibility, nor the apparent rational tangibility of formal obligations, will hinder the Christian endowed with true freedom of spirit in conforming himself to God's will.

Circumstance ethics, in its legitimate protest against the bureaucrat type who erroneously admits only formal obligations, itself falls prey to several grave errors.

First, it confuses general moral commandments, because of their precise formulation, with those commandments having the character of formal obligation. It overlooks the fact that the commandments of the Decalogue, for instance, "Thou shalt not kill," "Thou shalt not commit adultery," "Thou shalt honor thy father and thy mother," "Thou shalt not have strange gods before me," impose typically material obligations. The character of a clear formulation is confused with the juridical character.[12]

Second, the champions of circumstance ethics overlook the fact that even in those cases where the call of God has to be understood in a given situation without the help of a concretely formulated commandment, this call reveals itself precisely through the morally relevant values included in the situation.

In order to understand what corresponds to God's will, in a concrete situation when no concrete commandment indicates the way, and when we are relying exclusively upon the commandments of love of God and love of neighbor, we have to perceive the morally relevant values at stake. It is through them that we discover the way corresponding to these two basic commandments. These values are by their very nature general and the commandment issuing from them is also general.[13]

Third, circumstance ethics confuses the obligatory character of moral commandments with what we have termed formal obligation. The "demanding" character of the commandment is misinterpreted as a purely formal obligation or is at least seen in the light of it. Its exponents fall prey precisely to the confusion that we warned against before. This

---

[12] The absurdity of this confusion assumes a particularly drastic character when prohibitive commandments with an absolute veto are opposed as formal obligations to the call of charity. No call of a good—as high ranking as it may be—can ever supersede those commandments. We are never allowed to sin in order to do something good. The idea that any situation could arise in which we should, out of charity, disregard one of these commandments is plainly nonsensical. Cf. Chapter X, "Basic Errors of Circumstance Ethics."

[13] Cf. Chapter X, "Basic Errors of Circumstance Ethics."

leads them even to attempt to expel from morality the specific "oughtness" that is an essential feature of this sphere. In the name of fighting a legalistic morality, they offer a complete misinterpretation of morality and charity. This most important point will be discussed in detail in Chapter X.

Finally, they fail to appreciate the true moral character of formal obligations. They do not see that the formal obligation has its full moral significance, and that the fact that the bureaucrat overrates it or rather tends to make it the *causa exemplaris* of all morality does not affect the objective validity of formal obligation.

True freedom of spirit implies a clear sense of the hierarchy of values and of the rank of moral commandments. It means precisely that one is able to distinguish clearly between moral commandments with an absolute veto and moral commandments that can be superseded by others.

Thus, freedom of spirit is characterized equally by an unshakable obedience to all commandments with an absolute veto by a strict fulfillment of letter as well as spirit, and by a readiness, on the other hand, to depart from the letter of the commandments without absolute veto, as soon as a higher value calls for it. It is actually an absolute faithfulness to the spirit that makes the Christian possessing freedom of spirit adamant in all cases in which there is no possibility of fulfilling the spirit without obeying the letter, and that makes him supple in the matter of disregarding the letter where the spirit calls for it.

Thus Christian freedom of spirit is, on the one hand, the antithesis to all types of laxism, to jovial open-mindedness, to the so-called "wide conscience," to the bohemian disregard of formal obligations, and especially to the false freedom of circumstance ethics that wants to replace moral commandments by the voice of a blind conscience; and on the other hand, it is the antithesis to the bureaucrat's monomania for formal obligations and to the fettered attitude of the morally timorous man.

Circumstance ethics rightly protests against that tendency

to escape from full personal responsibility that is found in the morally timorous man, and, in a different way, in the pedant and the bureaucrat. In the case of the timorous man, it is a regrettable weakness, but in the case of the bureaucrat and pedant it is a grave moral perversion. What is characteristic of the moral bureaucrat is not his fear of deciding anything without being protected and "insured" all the way by formal prescriptions. It is rather a kind of spiritual laziness that refuses to go into the depths and to abandon oneself. The timorous man, on the contrary, shuns risk. The bureaucrat shuns the "personal"; he shuns the self-abandonment that a true value response implies. He shuns real co-operation with a value, letting oneself be "taken" by it.

The moral bureaucrat also has an antipathy toward the entire world of calls and obligations that are not classified under a clear-cut formula. An obligation dictated by charity seems to him nebulous, vague, and unsubstantial. He refuses to commit himself to this sphere, for no one can say where such commitment will lead. With mistrust, and even a kind of fear, he looks at it as if it were quicksand. He is too conventional to assume a real personal responsibility, although he has an exaggerated sense of responsibility for the fulfillment of the very letter of formal obligations.

Here again we must say that the protest of circumstance ethics against the escape from the *"risque personnel"* in the bureaucrat or the timorous type is certainly praiseworthy. But as soon as the "personal risk" begins to mean that one should ignore moral commandments in a moral decision, and even the morally relevant values at stake, a grave error comes to the fore. The attitude of reserving to our conscience alone the power to decide everything in a confrontation with God, yet eliminating any general principle or value, betrays a much more radical refusal of true self-abandonment than the attitude of the bureaucrat. The "personal risk" then assumes the character of a proud self-assertion and a lack of the *"timor Domini, initium sapientiae,"* the fear of God, which is the beginning of wisdom.

## Chapter VI

## *"FELIX CULPA"*

WE SAW before that circumstance ethics emphasizes that the tragic sinner who is aware of his sinfulness and suffers from it may be a morally better person, deeper, more humble, more charitable, loving God more than a self-righteous person who is in no open conflict with clearly formulated moral precepts. The proponents of this theory say that the sinner, once reconciled to God, will be more prepared for grace than the mediocre, correct person who is tainted with self-righteousness.

This judgment may be right. The Parable of the Pharisee and the Publican clearly reveals that humility is decisive in our moral life, that the humble sinner ranks higher than the pharisee, in other words, that the sin of pride, and especially of pharisaic pride, is worse than many other sins. It may be legitimate to extend this judgment analogically to the self-righteous man as well as to the pharisee. But in any case it implies that the publican is aware of his sin and rejects it, that he repents of his sin and at least intends to overcome it.

We must clearly understand and fully realize that the publican is not superior *because* of his sin, but in spite of it. He is superior because of his humility, because he is conscious of his sinfulness, because in fact he hates sin more than the pharisee does. The sin of the publican does not become morally good because his attitude is—in spite of his sin—morally noble after sinning.

It is a radical error to feel entitled to glorify sin on account of the Parable of the Pharisee and the Publican. The breathtaking revolution contained in this parable is the overwhelming, all-important role of humility and contrition. But sinning, as such, is not regarded as of little account, and still less is it glorified by this parable. On the contrary, the disvalue of sinning is presupposed. The horrible, momentous character of sinning is precisely the very background here against which the fathomless depth of humility reveals itself.

On the other hand, the Parable of the Publican does not make the nonrepentant, blunt sinner any less repulsive. For example, this parable could not be applied to the bad thief on the cross, and still less to a proud, satanic sinner like Cain.

We shall come back to the basic error of sin mysticism in Chapter VIII when dealing with the question of which factors may render the tragic or the noble sinner morally superior to the self-righteous man. In discussing the role that sin plays with regard to this superiority, the absurdity of any glorification of sin will reveal itself anew. Here we must throw into relief another grave error. Let us suppose that a man really has been morally awakened and morally deepened because of his fall. Let us imagine the case of a man who is deeply contrite after falling into sin. His regret leads him to a radical conversion, such as the one of Fra Cristoforo in Manzoni's *The Betrothed*. In this case, sinning was psychologically instrumental for his conversion. Though calling the sin "instrumental" for Fra Cristoforo's conversion, it is plainly not possible to decide whether he would not have been converted and raised to the same moral and religious level *without* sinning. It suffices to state that in *this* case, *de facto,* his fall was instrumental for his conversion. And thus we may speak in a certain way of a *"felix culpa,"* [1] a happy fault. But this is possible only in a retrospective view. As soon as we believe that because a sin *may* have, retrospectively speaking, the character of a *felix culpa,* we are entitled under special circumstances to sin,[2] or to advise an-

---

[1] St. Augustine, *City of God,* XIV, 13, 44: "And therefore I dare say it is good that the proud should fall into some broad and disgraceful sin."

[2] Patently, it is impossible ever to do something morally evil in order to be led by it to a deep contrition, and consequently to a conversion.

As soon as one considers contrition and the rejection of sin as desirable,

other person to sin, we fall prey to a grave and disastrous error.

It is of the *utmost importance* to distinguish clearly here between two basically different situations. The first refers to the moral decision that someone has to make in a given set of circumstances. It is concerned with the questions, "What shall I do from the moral point of view? What shall I choose?" It also embraces every piece of advice that I may give to another person when he is confronted with such a decision. The second refers to our moral judgment of other persons *after* they have acted. It is concerned with the moral evaluation of an established fact. Retrospectively speaking, it may be allowable to consider another person's sin as being a *"felix culpa,"* but to invite someone to sin with the hope of bringing about good moral results would be tantamount to advocating the odious principle that the end justifies the means.

The moral commandment implies an absolute veto of any sinful action insofar as our own decisions as well as our influence on other persons' decisions are concerned. No circumstance whatever, no end—sublime as it may be—should ever induce us to violate such a commandment. Even presuming the absurd possibility that we could convert all sinners

---

one *must* also reject one's present sin. To choose a sin as a means for attaining a deep contrition is intrinsically impossible if the very nature of contrition is understood. Only if one aspired to a sham contrition, a mere emotional state lacking all intentional response character, a pseudo contrition that is relished for its own sake, could one try to evoke this emotion by sinning. But it is obvious that this sham contrition is the very antithesis to true contrition. To choose sin in order to experience such a sham contrition is playing with God and killing the very core of any desire for true contrition. Even if someone would say he is not speaking of contrition, but of a moral awakening and a realization of one's misery and sinfulness and of the humility that will develop when one turns back onto the right path, the same impossibility is to be found. There is no moral awakening, no humility without a deep contrition, and thus it is likewise impossible to aspire to this awakening by means of sinning.

Cf. Rahner, Karl, S. J. *"Situations ethik und Suendenmystik,"* the passage that begins: *"Das Gott auf krummen Linien gerade schreiben kann, gibt der Kreatur kein Recht, krumme Linien im Buch ihres Lebens zu ziehen." Stimmen der Zeit,* 145 Band, Verlag Herder Freiburg, 1949–1950, p. 341 (That God can write straight with crooked lines does not entitle creatures to write crooked lines in the book of their lives.)

by committing a sin ourselves, we would never be allowed to choose this means for such a high moral end. St. Augustine says that if we could save all hell through a venial sin, we would not be allowed to commit it.

In the retrospective view, which *alone* entitles us to speak of a *"felix culpa,"* we quit, as it were, the realm of moral judgments and turn to a completely different level, the level of the mysterious ways of Providence. St. Augustine himself says that God manifests His grandeur nowhere more strikingly than in using evil for the good.[3]

It is one thing to look at man's life in the light of Providence, of God's inscrutable ways, and another to look at man's life in the light of what he should choose, of how he should decide, and of what he is morally bound to do and to omit.

The former aspect is essentially retrospective. It refers only to the past, since, obviously, the ways of Providence only manifest themselves to us in the past and are invisible as long as they belong to the future. We foresee causal effects and refer our actions to the future. But the dispensations of Providence—unforeseen and unforeseeable—belong to the opaque future. The fact that the ways of Providence are such, however, is not the reason why we are forbidden to choose or even to consider any sin as a *felix culpa*. Even if the ways of Providence were foreseeable, we would never be allowed to choose the "sin" that in God's plan would be a means for even great moral goods. A sin may be considered as *"felix"* only in retrospective view, because in calling a sin a *"felix culpa"* we never include any judgment concerning the moral disvalue of the sin, even if the *"felix"* refers to a moral improvement. The sin does not lose its intrinsic moral disvalue by the fact that God's infinite mercy permitted it to become a starting point for moral improvement. The term *"felix"* does not deny the intrinsic moral disvalue of the fault and the

---

[3] St. Augustine, *The City of God*, XXII, 1, p. 358: "He (God) did not deprive them of this power (free will) knowing it a more powerful thing to make good use of such as were evil, than to exclude evil altogether."

offense against God contained in it. It must never influence our position toward sinning or diminish our horror of it.

Finally, the *felix culpa* aspect is possible only as pertaining to others and not to one's own person. Looking back at our own past sin, if it was objectively a *felix culpa*, as in the case of Fra Cristoforo, one has always primarily to repent of it, and this forbids our considering it as a *felix culpa*. Here the fact that it turned out to be the starting point for our conversion can only present itself in the light of God's ineffable mercy, and not in the light of a *felix culpa*. It never could lead to our saying, "I am glad that I sinned because through that I found God." Retrospectively we may say of another person that we are glad that he fell, if this was instrumental for his conversion. But with respect to ourselves, the regret essentially immanent to contrition excludes such an approach. Here the wish that we had never offended God remains the basic position toward our former sin and coexists with gratitude for God's mercy, which freed us in spite of our sin.

Thus, we can clearly see that it is of the utmost importance to understand the conditions under which alone we may speak of a *felix culpa*. It is possible only in a retrospective view and only with respect to other persons. The *felix culpa* can in no way whatever change our position toward sin as such. It can in no way weaken or dissolve the absolute veto implied in moral commandments, and thus it can never influence our own moral decisions, or our advice in relation to the moral decisions of others. To derive from the possibility of a *felix culpa* the right to choose, under extraordinary circumstances, a sinful action, is one of the basic errors that we find in circumstance ethics, at least in its most radical form.[4]

The following must be stressed with all possible emphasis. Necessary as it is to insist on the overwhelming role of hu-

---

[4] A typical case of this error is to be found in Le Fort's *Kranz der Engel*. The Father Angelo who advises Veronica to accept a marriage outside the Church because in doing so she may eventually succeed in converting her fiancé, patently adheres to the principle, "The end justifies the means." He advises her to commit a sin in order to attain eventually an end of great value.

mility and the moral evil of self-righteousness and mediocrity and legitimate as it may be to prefer the noble or tragic sinner to the self-righteous man, whether zealot or mediocrity, our position toward moral commandments, whether in regard to our own decisions or our advice to others, can *in no way* be modified. The absolute veto, forbidding us ever to choose something sinful, remains unchanged by the fact that the tragic sinner may rank higher as a person than the self-righteous man. We thus cannot sufficiently deplore the fact that the truly Christian tendency to stress the horror of self-righteousness and mediocrity and to unmask the mediocre correctness of the self-righteous man in his hypocrisy and emptiness has led in certain exponents to what is the very antithesis of Christian morality, namely, to the principle that the end justifies the means:

It is not allowed to do evil in order that good may result from it (Cf. Romans, 3:8), but this ethics acts—perhaps without being aware of it—according to the principle that the end justifies the means.[5]

---

[5] Allocution of Pope Pius XII to the Fédération Mondiale des Jeunesses Féminines Catholiques, *L'Osservatore Romano,* April, 1952.

CHAPTER VII

PERSON AND ACTION

In *Christian Ethics,* we stressed that there are three different fields in which the moral life of man displays itself, or in which man can be endowed with moral values or stained by moral disvalues, namely, actions, affective responses and acts, and the habitual qualities of the personality. We not only differentiated among these three fields, but we emphasized that each of them has its own full significance and that we cannot reduce one to the other, as has indeed often been attempted. The good action and the evil action have their full moral significance and import. The action is a full moral reality and not merely an indicator of the moral character of a personality. Likewise, virtues are a full actualization of moral values and not only a disposition for eventual, morally good actions.

Circumstance ethics, while reacting against an overstressing of action as such, tends to deny the full significance of actions and to consider them only as indices of one's moral standard. Its champions deny that an action has any definite moral character, claiming that it receives a moral significance only through the entire moral standard of one's individual personality.

The tendency to give to morality a specifically juridical character by reducing morality to mere conformity with certain moral prescriptions for acting is certainly deplorable. It depersonalizes morality by overlooking the role of the entire personality in the moral sphere and by contenting itself with mere conformity to general rules of our acting, as though one were desirous of nothing more than a certificate of good conduct. A threefold mistake is included in this approach. First, the full significance of the entire moral standard of a person is neglected—the sphere of virtues and vices. Second, the moral superiority of this sphere is overlooked. Third, the role of the person's character for the moral significance of the action is not taken into account.

On the other hand, it is a grave error to disregard the moral significance of an action as such and its role in the entire person. This grave neglect is to be found precisely in circumstance ethics. However, we must not only see that each of these three fields has a moral significance of its own, but we also must understand that they are closely interwoven.

It is especially the relation between the single action and the character of the individual personality that forms the crucial point in the interpretation of morality in juridical terms on the one hand, and on the other in terms of circumstance ethics. Granted that the degree of responsibility for an evil action and the illumination and background of this action depend on the general moral character of a person, it is a terrible error not to see that the evil action, as such, affects the entire moral status of a person. Apart from the moral impact that the evil action possesses in itself, it also stains the *whole* person to such an extent that it separates him in a specific way from God as long as the sinful action has not been repented of and has not been pardoned by God. It renders the person guilty. Granted that it makes a great difference whether or not the sinner is a morally good and morally deep person, whether or not he has morally a basically good intention, whether or not it is a David who has fallen or a Cain, the fact remains that through a sinful action David, the noble, the great David, is stained and guilty. A barrier is erected by an evil action, and it commits man as an entire personality, even if through his evil action he does not lose every morally noble quality of his character, especially, for example, all its potential depth and goodness.

Circumstance ethics claims that in the name of personalism we must consider the person as a whole, that we must also take into account the fact that because a human person's being is extended in time, we are not allowed to cling to one isolated action in our evaluations. Certainly our moral judgment of a person must not limit itself to the sphere of action. It must also, while deploring an evil action, consider the entire character of the sinner, his general dispositions, the basic direction of his will, and all his eventual virtues. But the fact that all these other dimensions still exist in a personality in no way effaces the decisive commitment that came into existence through the evil action. The extension of a person's life in time justifies the contention that we can never express a definite judgment on him as long as he lives. But it can never justify the denial that every single action has a definite moral character, that an evil action constitutes a full, "valid" reality, or that it commits the entire person. To grant time such a role, to consider the person as being in no moment capable of performing fully valid acts, amounts to the denial of one of the deepest and most essential features of man as a person. This stand dispossesses man of one of the essential foundations of his dignity, namely, the capacity of committing himself in one act. It also overlooks the relation existing between time and eternity, the way in which morality transcends time and reaches into eternity. It forgets the position of man between time and eternity, and the fact that a moral guilt never becomes superannuated or inveterate.

The true relation between the single action and the person is admirably disclosed in the Church's conception of sin. On the one hand, the last word about a person's moral standard is never spoken as long as he lives because in the last moment he can always either be converted, like the good thief on the cross, or become an apostate. The role of time in the person's existence is thus fully taken into account. On the other hand, the full moral validity of an action is equally emphasized in the Church's stressing that a single mortal sin separates man from God, depriving him of the state of grace, whatever his moral standard may be. And the separation from God lasts as long as the sin is unrepented, unconfessed, and unpardoned through the sacrament of penance. Even if the sin is not repeated and if the same person performs many good actions, the separation from God remains.

We see how erroneous it is to underrate the moral significance of single actions, even if the original intention underlying this attitude is a desire to emphasize the moral significance of an individual's lasting qualities. Necessary as it is to see the moral significance of the person's character, his lasting and habitual qualities, his virtues and vices, his basic direction of will, we must never fall into the terrible error of underrating the moral significance of single actions or of misconceiving their power of commitment.

Here again a grave error of circumstance ethics comes to the fore. Starting with the desire to emphasize personality and to fight against the depersonalization of morality that results from focusing exclusively on actions as such, champions of circumstance ethics end by becoming blind to the moral impact of an action and to the specific dignity of man's nature as a person, which manifests itself precisely in his capacity to commit himself by his actions.

In considering King David, we clearly see that notwithstanding his terrible sin (adultery coupled with indirect murder), in his basic moral attitude he still clearly differs from Cain. In falling, he did not completely give up his faith or his love of God. The moral potential of his personality did not fade away. As we can see, in his case there are yet many levels and deeper strata in which a sense of moral values is still alive. This is clearly revealed in his attitude when the Prophet Nathan tells him the story of the rich man and of the poor man who owned but one lamb. He immediately responds with full moral indignation. He not only grasps the moral disvalue involved, but the story also fills his soul with horror in regard to the attitude described to him. It is in this disposition that he hears the words of Nathan, "Thou art this man," whereupon he turns completely back to God in his contrition.

This event in David's life admirably reveals two fundamental facts: on the one hand, the full moral significance of the evil action itself, and, on the other, the full moral significance of the lasting qualities of the person and the impossibility of restricting moral judgment to the sphere of actions and of ignoring the complexity of the whole person and the stratum of habitual qualities.

Yet circumstance ethics does not minimize the sphere of action merely in order to stress that deeper stratum in the person wherein we find superactual attitudes and virtues. In stressing only the sincere intention in which one follows the voice of one's conscience before God, the radical exponents of circumstance ethics also desubstantialize superactual attitudes and virtues. Both terms, "sincere intention" and "conscience," are, however, ambiguous. First, intention may refer to the will underlying an action. In this sense we may say of an action that it was against our intention when the action is the opposite of what we intended and believed we were doing. By mistake a man may give a sick person a deadly poison instead of the helpful medicine that he believes it to be. Here the discrepancy is due to a purely factual error. The real happening is in strict contradiction to our will. Intention in this sense patently determines the entire moral character of an action. Secondly, in distinguishing intention and action, we may refer by intention to the motive underlying an action and to a motive that may be opposed to the moral character that the action possesses as such. In this case there is no discrepancy between the person's image of the situation and action and the situation and action as they exist in reality. There is no discrepancy due to a factual error, as in the former case. Here the discrepancy is a result of a value blindness. The intention is, as such, a value response, directed to a real good endowed with morally relevant values, but the individual in this case believes that only the motive endows an action with its moral character, and thus feels entitled to disobey moral commandments because of this noble intention. Such is the case of Sonja,[1] or of a man who perpetrates euthanasia out of compassion, or who interrupts

[1] Cf. Chapter III, "The Tragic Sinner."

gestation in order to save the life of a mother. Traditional philosophy would characterize intention in this sense as *"finis operantis"* as against *"finis operis."*

If one says that intention alone in the first case counts before God, one is right, because it determines exclusively the moral character of the action. This has always been admitted by saying that ignorance of facts suspends responsibility, granted that the error does not result from carelessness. But to claim that "intention" in the second sense alone counts, as circumstance ethics does, is a grave error, as we have pointed out several times.

Yet circumstance ethics sometimes goes much further. It uses "intention" in a third sense, in which it means an obedience to our conscience that is in no way orientated to general moral principles or morally relevant values. Here its proponents deny the response character of intention.

Every intention must be a response to a good, and its moral value depends upon whether this good is endowed with morally relevant values and whether or not the intention is motivated by these values. We shall see in Chapter IX, that in ousting all general moral commandments and all morally relevant values, which are by their very nature general, the intention that, according to them, follows exclusively the dictate of our own conscience has lost its object and is thus deprived of all qualitative characteristics. A conscience that is not based on the knowledge of morally relevant values and disvalues is deprived of its very capacity to inform us about the morally right way we are to follow. A conscience that is not "fed" by moral commandments and by grasping morally relevant and moral values is a blind conscience. Actually, is is an impossible fiction.[2]

[2] This will become clear in Chapter X, where we shall discuss the nature of "conscience" and its ambiguous use in circumstance ethics.

## Chapter VIII

## SIN MYSTICISM

It is certainly true that pharisaism in the mitigated form of self-righteousness is one of the main dangers in the Christian's moral and spiritual life. It is a specifically great danger because, unlike other forms of pride, it does not present itself to one's mind as a rebellion against morality. Other forms of pride are in open rivalry with the fulfillment of the moral commandments, for example, the pride of the ambitious man who strives for power and fame. Such pride incites one to neglect or to violate a moral commandment in order to attain one's goal. Napoleon was fully aware, in ordering the execution of the Duke of Enghien, that his ambition was inciting him to commit a crime. The pride of the man who resents bowing before a moral commandment or submitting to a God-given authority leads to a clear conflict with the moral sphere, which cannot but become conscious in a Christian striving for moral perfection. Even the haughtiness that bars one's asking forgiveness for a wrong done to another person is clearly experienced as inimical to our striving to fulfill God's commandments.

Pharisaic trends, on the contrary, can creep into our souls without making us aware of the glaring conflict with moral commandments and with God. This type of pride can steal in while we are concentrated on obedience to those moral commandments that refer to actions.

Certainly, every Christian is aware of the danger of pride as such and of the moral evil implied or included in an open self-glorification. Everyone knows the temptation accompanying the performance of a good action. Such was the temptation experienced by St. Bernard, who while preaching, suddenly began marveling at his talent as an orator. He counteracted this upsurge of pride by saying, "Satan, I did not begin to preach for thee; for thee I will not cease to do it."

The danger of pharisaic trends is more subtle. It is not simply a transient temptation of moral pride as in the case of St. Bernard. It is a deeper, habitual type of pride, which can even coexist with an energetic suppression of open, proud, momentary temptations. The deep, habitual self-righteousness that makes one "judge" others as if one were a *defensor fidei* is much less obvious to our conscience than momentary temptations of moral pride.

If pride in our moral values is specifically grave, it would be wrong to believe, however, that it always has a pharisaic taint. The tendency to look back with pride when we have done something morally good—either rejoicing in a self-complacent way or even in a kind of self-glorification—is a general tendency in our fallen nature. This continuous danger, of which we are more easily aware, differs clearly from the danger of self-righteousness tainted with pharisaism.

The self-righteous attitude is a habitual and general one. It concerns the way in which a man habitually feels his own state of being, the way in which he approaches life and especially other persons. In its habitual character, it displays itself in a deeper stratum than does an attack of moral pride in a single situation. Self-righteousness does not refer so much to a single action as to one's general moral standard. Characteristically enough, the pharisee of the parable says, "I thank thee, God, that I am not like this sinner."

Apart from its habitual character, self-righteousness is characterized by its moral security. Specifically, the self-righteous man is sure of his moral status; he assumes a certain kind of *infallibility*. He not only rejoices over his moral goodness—which a merely self-complacent man may also do—but he feels himself firmly and solidly rooted in his moral correctness, sheltered and protected within his moral fortress. The security of the self-righteous man makes him "judge" everyone and everything. The morally vain man does not necessarily "judge." He is satisfied with his own perfection and may even have a tendency to believe too easily that other persons are morally good. The self-complacent, morally vain man can be a gentle person, friendly, goodhearted, and jovial. The self-righteous man in his character of a "judge" is hard. He enjoys being indignant and relishes sentencing others. In this lies his affinity with the pharisee.

The experience of an open conflict with moral commandments may prevent self-righteousness from arising, by humiliating the sinner and reminding him of his weakness and of his dependence upon God's help.

It is this fact that has led to the confusion at the basis of circumstance ethics and sin mysticism. The horror of pharisaism, of any pharisaic taint, tends to degenerate into indulgence toward sin. Sometimes it even creates a "sin mysticism," which projects into sin a kind of mysterious depth, a halo of humility, as though sin itself were a protection against pharisaism.

The hard, hypocritical sentence that the self-righteous man inflicts on the sinner evokes as it were a reaction of protective indulgence toward the sinner. This is understandable in a concrete situation with respect to an individual sinner. But there is no basis for it when applied to sins as such. The falseness and mercilessness of the self-righteous attitude stains only the self-righteous person, but it *does not cleanse* the sinner. Because of the sin of the self-righteous individual, the sin of the man whom he enjoys condemning does not cease to be a sin.

This fact must be borne clearly in mind. Every sin, as we saw, is intrinsically ugly and incompatible with the love of God. In every sin there is a germ of opposition to the love of God and to charity—a germ of that which in pharisaism stares at us in a refined and specific way.

Sin, as such, has nothing about it that justifies any indulgence—not to mention glorification. Far from possessing any antithesis to pharisaism, sin shares with it the feature of immorality. We must not forget that pharisaism is repulsive because it is a *great sin*.

It is true that consciousness of one's sinfulness is opposed to pharisaism. It might even be conceded that psychologically this consciousness is more likely to fade away if someone has never undergone serious trials in his life. Yet, *it must emphatically be said* that sinning, as such, is in no way a protection against pharisaism.

We have stressed several times that it is impossible to *oppose* the self-righteous man to the tragic sinner, forgetting that, in such a case, we are opposing one type of sinner to another. We have now to emphasize that the real antithesis to pharisaism and all forms of self-righteousness is to be found in the humility and charity that we find in a saint. The saint—and not the tragic sinner—is the antithesis to the pharisee and the self-righteous man. Humility necessarily implies a consciousness of our sinfulness and imperfection, but clearly it does not presuppose sinning, a blatant disobedience of any moral commandment. In the saints we find the deepest and most vivid consciousness of their unworthiness and sinfulness—notwithstanding the fact that they abstain from sinning. They clearly testify to the fact that humility in no way presupposes sin, and that it is a grave error to deal with sin as the antithesis of pharisaism and self-righteousness.

Moreover, we must stress that though humility is, as St. Francis de Sales says, the highest virtue—apart from charity—there exist also other virtues, such as purity, justice, and meekness. We need only recall the Sermon on the Mount in order to realize that.

In every sin, in every disobedience in regard to a moral commandment, in any neglect of morally relevant goods, in any action or attitude endowed with a moral disvalue, there is an element either of concupiscence or of pride, generally of both. It is ultimately always the same evil spirit of irreverence, rebellion, antagonism to God and the world of moral values that shows its ugly visage in a specifically hideous way in the pharisee and in a more mitigated form in the self-righteous man.

Great as are the differences in the realm of moral evil, manifold as are the levels in the hierarchy of moral evil, one cannot fight the devil in the name of Beelzebub. One cannot see in the tragic sinner the antipode of the self-righteous man or make of sinning an antidote to pharisaism.

It is not sin that is opposed to pharisaism, but the self-humiliation that is implied in contrition and that is even included in the sorrowful realization of one's weakness and in the humility implied in the appeal to God's mercy.

The Christian who abstains from grave sin out of his love for Christ is necessarily aware of his frailty and sinfulness. He possesses precisely, *a fortiori,* the advantage that a tragic sinner may have with respect to a self-righteous man—but without sinning. We shall understand this better after having analyzed more in detail which element places the tragic sinner as a person morally above the self-righteous man.

Let us first take the case of the noble sinner, for example, Sonja, in Dostoievski's *Crime and Punishment.* We have already discussed the specific nature of this case. Now we want to emphasize that it is her heroic, subjective intention that endows her with a high moral value, in spite of her objective sin.

Sonja is noble and great because of her heroic charity, her readiness to sacrifice the *intimum* of her personal life, to annihilate herself, as it were, and to accept the most horrible humiliation, in order to help her suffering family. But she could as well possess this moral splendor without committing a deplorable sin, without falling prey to a grave moral error, even to a moral value blindness. Not only did she possess the same deep charity, the same heroic nobility before she fell prey to this error, but this charity and heroism could have led her to make other sacrifices, in which all these moral values would shine forth—sacrifices that would, however, in no way imply sin.

Her moral nobility is not only independent of her sinning, but it clearly exists in spite of her sinning. Her moral error, her underlying value blindness, betrays the fact that *certain* moral imperfections are to be found in her. Later on, Sonja overcomes precisely these deplorable moral shortcomings. But in spite of her moral error and her objective sin, Sonja is a great and lovable moral personality, one who deserves our loving esteem. Here it is obvious that her objective sinning is not even a *felix culpa*, for it is in no way instrumental to her attaining a higher moral standard. It is not even her consciousness of sin or her contrition that elevate her in such an extraordinary way. She does not even understand that her "sacrifice" was sinful. She was humble before sinning, her inner attitude was the very opposite of self-righteousness, although she certainly never had gravely sinned before. The extraordinary paradox in this case is that such noble moral attitudes are, through a moral error, invested in an objectively sinful way of acting.

Sonja's sinning is so far from being indispensable for the unfolding of these noble attitudes, so far from being in any way instrumental or in any way even linked to it psychologically, that we must deplore her moral error, wishing she had not invested all this noble moral treasure in an objectively horrible sin.

In this case of the noble sinner, the impossibility of giving any positive indirect function to sin is so obvious that it lies beyond the problem at stake in circumstance ethics and in sin mysticism.[1]

---

[1] Every attempt to interpret the case of Sonja on the assumption that she chose to join the sinners, to accept the burden of sin out of charity, is clearly impossible. Sonja would never have decided to become a prostitute if she had understood that she was morally not allowed to make this sacrifice, that she sinned in doing so, even if any impure motive was fully absent and she had a horror of doing it. Her pious, Christ-loving attitude would never have consented to sin in order to do good. The principle of "the end justifies the means" is precisely the terrible error of Raskolnikov, which she tries to explain to him as being an error. She sees only, on the one hand, the greatest personal sacrifice, the most terrible humiliation, and on the other hand, the terrible emergency of her family, and, subjectively, she believes

Let us now turn to the completely different case of the tragic sinner, which we mentioned before. In the category of the tragic sinner, we want to study first the case of a man who deeply and passionately loves a divorced woman. They are both Catholics; and the circumstances are such that if they marry they commit a grave sin. They are aware of the terrible conflict in which their love places them. On the one side is their earthly happiness; on the other is the commandment of God, of the God Whom they love and Whom they want to obey. They experience their helplessness, their misery, and they ardently beg God to help them. But finally they fall. In their despair, they consent to sin. They feel they are great sinners and are miserable, but they also believe they have invested the best of their personalities in their mutual love. The more complete union seems to them something noble and great. They feel too weak to sacrifice it and turn to God, praying that He may show them a way out of their conflict. This case clearly differs from the case of Sonja. No moral error is here the reason of their fall. Thus it cannot be said that in the case of the sinful marriage the partners acted morally well subjectively. It is obvious that they sinned not only objectively but subjectively as well. Their action, as such, contains no positive moral elements. If it is permitted to say that *relatively* they may have more love of God than the self-righteous zealot, that they may have a greater charity and humility than the self-righteous, mediocre, correct man [2] who is in no flagrant conflict with a moral commandment, it is clearly not *because* of their sin, but only *in spite* of it. Their mutual love may be a deep and noble one, the potential of love in both may exhibit the depth and ardor of their personalities, but this love could also be present if no conflict with a moral commandment had arisen. The fact that one loves a divorced woman certainly adds nothing to the depth and nobility of this love. And this love could

---

that she is accepting a sacrifice that God demands from her. But she does not understand that God forbids what she is doing.

[2] Cf. pp. 95–96.

have been just as great and deep if the lovers had renounced marriage rather than offend God. Indeed, their love would not only have been just as deep, it would have been much deeper if, notwithstanding their ardor and tenderness, they had understood that a union, against God's will, *is in fact a separation,* that instead of uniting lovers, sinning in common tears them asunder.[3]

We see, therefore, that whatever is positive in their love, draws on our sympathy, and manifests a noble basic attitude is in no way linked to their sin, but exists only in spite of this sin.

The same must be said of the grave conflict in which they find themselves. Let us grant that this conflict shakes them to the very depth of their souls, that it forces them off the superficial level on which a self-righteous correct man who has no experience of a grave conflict may remain. But this awakening experience is still not linked to sin. They would also have had this experience if they had had the strength to avoid sin by making the great sacrifice. Moreover, let us repeat: if—given the same intensity, ardor, and depth of mutual love—they had abstained from sinning, renouncing the fulfillment of their deepest earthly happiness, they would have reached an incomparably greater depth and would have experienced an incomparably fuller awakening.

Let us now compare the tragic sinner with a mediocre, correct man who is not self-righteous, but who is superficial and preoccupied with peripheral earthly things, such as his social position, wealth, etc. The absence of grave sins is not yet an absolute guarantee of the presence of moral virtues. It may be that a man has never committed a gravely immoral action because he never was tempted to do so, having always lived in happy circumstances, being well off, and without worries, and having no violent passions. Such a man, having no great aspirations, is satisfied as long as he is allowed to live an unhindered life in which he can enjoy his different

---

[3] Cf. D. von Hildebrand, *"Virtus Unitiva der Werte," Metaphysik der Gemeinschaft* (Augsburg: Hass und Grabherr).

hobbies. He has never undergone trials that have tested his basic moral attitude or his love of God. He is neither specifically proud nor humble; he possesses a good portion of selfishness; he is superficial and rather indifferent.

But patently it is not because the tragic sinner has committed a sin that he is a deeper, nobler personality than this mediocre, correct man. On the contrary, if he is this kind of personality, it is not because of his sinning, but in spite of it.

The only thing that can be said is that the correct mediocre man who is not self-righteous *may* rank in some respects morally lower than the tragic sinner. But this means primarily that the correctness is not always a guarantee of the presence of morally positive attitudes. And thus it may even be that a tragic sinner ranks higher insofar as he possesses some morally positive attitudes that the correct man lacks. But this fact in no way lessens the gravity of the tragic sinner's fault; it makes it in a certain way especially deplorable. The antithesis of tragic sinner and mediocre, correct man does not in reality elevate the tragic sinner, but it discloses the fact that the correct man may rank still lower as a personality.[4]

The same applies to the tragic sinner who is prey to a vice—the drunkard, for example—that he hates and against which he struggles, but without succeeding in overcoming it.[5] Here the humanly noble motive of the former tragic sinner is absent. Nevertheless, it may be true that he has a

[4] But it must emphatically be stressed that to abstain from sinning has a primacy with respect to performing good works. This primacy does not mean that it ranks higher as such, but that it is the first manifestation of our love of God, since the obligation to abstain from sinning must be fulfilled first in case of conflict. Our first—we are not referring to the order of time—concern must be not to offend God, and then come all works in which we realize goods having a morally relevant value, such as almsgiving, taking care of the sick, etc. This priority discloses itself in the fact that we never are allowed to commit a sin in order to do something good. We are not allowed to steal in order to help a poor man. St. Augustine says: "The order whereof (of virtue) is, first to do no man hurt, and secondly, to help all that he can." *The City of God*, XIX, 14 (Healey, *op. cit.*, p. 252).

[5] I am thinking only of cases in which a full responsibility is at stake. It is generally recognized today that to a large degree alcoholism is a disease.

deeper love of God and a greater humility than the correct man who is not in the grip of such a vice. But again we must say that it is not because of his sin that he ranks higher, but in spite of it.

We touch on something that seems more closely linked to sinning, stressing that the tragic sinner may have a consciousness of his helplessness, that he may be aware of his sinfulness and suffer deeply from his separation from God, and that he may cry out of his very depth: *"Miserere mei, Domine"*—a world of experience from which the zealot, the mediocre self-righteous man, and even the mediocre, correct man are excluded.

Yet if we examine reality more closely, even this awareness of one's sinfulness is in no way due to sinning. There are many cases of tragic sinners who through their sinning become even more blunted, losing—precisely *because* of their sinning—their consciousness of helplessness and sinfulness. Their conscience becomes darkened and indifferent because their pride tries to excuse their fall.

Whether or not this happens will depend largely upon the moral personality of the tragic sinner. The less such progressive moral degeneration takes place, the more we can assume that humility, moral wakefulness, and absence of self-righteous tendencies already existed in the tragic sinner before his sin.

We prescind here from the mystery of conversion through God's grace, which may make a St. Paul out of a Saul of Tarsus, and which may always occur after sinning, though obviously not through sinning. It can then be said that the general moral attitude that makes a certain kind of sinner tragic and distinguishes him from a mean, blunt, mediocre sinner does not result from sinning, for it was already present before the sin took place. Indeed, it was not only present before, but it is actually diminished through his fall, which counteracted it. In spite of being shattered and drawn into the full drama of morality, the tragic sinner has abandoned God and bowed before sin. The aspect of tragedy must not deceive us in regard to the intrinsic ugliness of sinning. We must beware of projecting into the case of a tragic sinner something of the venerableness of the guiltless sufferer. Every man who suffers innocently is, as it were, surrounded with the *aura* of venerableness. Through the Cross of Christ, every man who innocently suffers reflects in some faint way the glory of the Cross and calls for our reverent respect.[6] Yet this in no way applies to the suffering that derives from a sin that one has not yet given up and really repented of, turning back into the loving, merciful arms of God.

Not only the sinner who suffers because of the intrinsic disharmony of sin is excluded from his venerableness, but the tragic sinner as well. His suffering is the suffering of being separated from God by his own fault, by having freely disobeyed His commandments—a separation that could be terminated if the sinner took the hand that God's mercifulness offers him. The tragic sinner deserves our compassion and sympathy, but in no way the awe and respect to which the bearer of a cross is entitled. The suffering of the tragic sinner is precisely the consequence of the fact that he declined to accept the cross that God laid on him, or that he refused to endure the kind of suffering that confers on the bearer this mysterious venerability. If in our case of the two lovers they had renounced all earthly happiness, if they had permitted their hearts to be crucified rather than sin, then and then alone would their cross have an awe-inspiring character.

We saw before that in the case of a drunkard also the continual experience of his insufficiency and weakness, the humiliation resulting from repeated falls, and his deep sorrow about his sinfulness, may place him definitely higher than a self-righteous or mediocre correct man. Yet in claiming it is thanks to his sinning that he is mindful of his sinfulness and remains humble, one forgets that the overwhelming majority of drunkards manifest neither great charity nor humility, and that the normal effect of vice is a gradual proc-

[6] Patently this applies in a quite new and much more authentic sense to the one who endures his suffering in the spirit and imitation of Christ.

ess of moral blunting, a paralyzing of our moral striving, an indifference toward the moral sphere, a vanishing of any consciousness of sinfulness.

In order that such a vice—and only certain vices are in question in the framework of tragic sin, as we saw before—can have an effect of rendering a man aware of his sinfulness and of making him humble, he must already be endowed with a noble basic moral attitude. He must love God more than does the self-righteous man, and be humble, in order to avoid the blunting and morally decomposing effect of his vice. In short, he can preserve both his love of God to a certain extent and his more awakened conscience despite his sinning because he possessed them already before he fell. All that can be said here is that *even* a vice of this kind need not do away with all of one's moral values.

Yet, let us not forget that between his sorrow about his sinful state, his yielding to it in a kind of despair, and a real struggle against it, implying a full condemnation, a chasm yawns. The drunkard who really struggles to overcome his vice, whose fight is a fully serious one, will always go to confession and try anew to overcome it. But the one who only worries about his sinning but does not return to the house of his Father to beg for forgiveness, with the firm will to abstain from falling again, may deserve our compassion and sympathy, but he is not entitled to any respect for his suffering. Whereas the repentant sinner opens his hand to God's merciful clasp, the tragic sinner merely clasps his own hands in a despairing, passive resignation.

Disobeying any moral commandment is in no way a protection against the sin of self-righteousness. Sinning does not always have the humbling effect that may counteract self-righteousness. We have to go further yet. It is not only true that normally sinning leads to general moral decay and to the silencing of our conscience; but it is also true that sinning in no way excludes self-righteousness and other pharisaic tendencies, for there are people who are in grave conflict with moral commandments and are simultaneously self-righteous.

We shall first see that it is wrong to ascribe to sin a humbling effect that would render a man aware of his sinfulness and of his need for mercy. Second, we shall see that many people combine other sins with the sin of self-righteousness.

The only sinner who suffers moral humiliation is the one who is fully aware of the sinful character of his action and who in addition has an intention of avoiding sin, that is, a morally positive direction of the will. Sins that are not understood to be such, have, patently, no humbling effect. Even when sins are in some way known as immoral, if the sinner's basic intention is morally indifferent or even antimoral, these sins will have no humbling effect. For Don Giovanni and for Don Rodrigo, sin, far from humiliating them, rather increases their pride. (Efficiency in sinning can become a source of pride!)

Even in the case of a man who is not morally value-blind and who has a certain basic will to avoid morally evil things, though on a relatively mediocre level, not every kind of sinning may have a humbling effect, waking him up to the fact of his moral frailty and his need for divine help.

In speaking of the humbling effect of sin, we have to distinguish between humiliation in the sense of an injury to our pride, and humiliation in the sense of a self-humbling. Humiliation in the former sense is entailed in any failure or in one's cutting a bad or ridiculous figure. This humiliation in no way leads us necessarily to humility; it can create, rather, an inferiority complex, bitterness, desire of revenge. In short, it may harden pride instead of dissolving it. It has no relation to morality as such. A man can even be humiliated in this sense by not succeeding in a sinful undertaking.

This kind of humiliation often arises, if one is caught in the act of sinning, through the shame one feels when others know about one's insufficiency, inefficiency, or moral weakness. In this sense of "humiliation," sins are not humiliating in the full moral sense. They humiliate an individual only insofar as they affect his social image by damaging his reputation or insofar as he is ashamed of having his sin exposed to the light of day. Or sinning may humiliate him insofar as he tries futilely to overcome certain faults. But normally this humiliation has no morally awakening effect. Often God also uses such humiliation for a conversion.[7] But from a psychological point of view it cannot in any way have such effects.[8]

But this kind of humiliation is not that which is the issue in the sinning praised by circumstance ethics and sin mysticism as being instrumental to a moral deepening and to the counteracting of pride and self-righteousness. It is the humiliation that is understood as an experience that topples us from the pedestal of false moral security, awakening us to our sinfulness and our dependence upon God's grace. But, as we saw above, this "wholesome" humiliation already presupposes a basic direction toward the morally good and a sincere desire to avoid sin.[9]

[7] Such was the case in the life of St. Alfonso de Liguori, when the humiliation of losing a case he was defending in court was instrumental to his leaving the world.

[8] One could pose the question: "Which sins are humiliating in this sense?" More specifically, "Which sins are humiliating by being committed, and which sins are so when they become known to others?"

To our first question we must answer: It is less the specific type of sin that counts than the fact of how far the sin contradicts the ideal image we have of ourselves. The man who mainly wants to be reasonable, self-controlled, calm, superior to all situations, will be humiliated, for instance, if he loses his temper or if he becomes intoxicated, because this contradicts his ideal of himself. Another will be primarily humiliated by sexual sin because it belongs to the ideal of himself to be pure, spiritual, master of his senses.

To the second question, it must be said that indeed certain sins have a more humiliating effect. In general one is more ashamed of all sins of concupiscence when they become known to others than of sins deriving from pride. In the frame of sins motivated by concupiscence, one is more ashamed if these sins belong to the sphere of bodily concupiscence than if they are born of covetousness or avariciousness.

[9] It must be said that all general evil trends, such as lack of charity, habitual vanity, "self-evident" egotism, which make us push our interests into the foreground without even questioning the possibility of acting differently, register less easily in our conscience than single actions, which are in glaring contradiction to moral commandments, for instance, an impure

Yet this wholesome humiliation, leading to an awareness of our sinfulness and moral frailty, may already take place in the experience of temptation. Someone who is tempted by the flesh and who victoriously resists, undergoes a wholesome humiliation through the very experience of temptation. He becomes aware of his sinfulness and of the abyss separating him from the purity and holiness to which he is called by God's grace. The salutary humiliation that protects us from self-righteousness and awakens us from a mediocre, superficial correctness does not normally result from falling and sinning, but from the experience of temptation.

The drama of morality discloses itself to our mind precisely in the struggle against temptation, in the tension between our will animated by love of God and the susceptibility of our nature to the appeal of sinful things. It has often been stressed that the great moral resurrection that takes place through a deep and true contrition awakens us to the full grandeur and depth of the moral drama. But the struggle to overcome a temptation with the help of God's grace can imply the same love of God, the same break-through to the full realization of the moral drama, the same humiliation, the same consciousness of our frailty and of God's mercy.

Yet in speaking of temptation, we must try to eliminate some possible misunderstandings. The temptations we are thinking of are not evil tendencies of our nature, such as avariciousness, envy, lechery, sadism, but rather those arising in situations we are placed in, where there is an appeal to

action or theft. Sinning through habitual attitudes is more apt to remain unobserved. These sins often belong to those the Psalmist refers to in saying: "*Ab occultis meis, munda me.*" They lead, therefore, less to real humiliation. They rarely present themselves to our conscience in so drastic a manner as to have this humiliating effect. But if suddenly they are fully revealed to our mind as in conversion (Staretz Zossima in Dostoievski's *Brothers Karamazov*), they are above all humiliating in this wholesome, deep sense of the term. Here also the humiliation may greatly depend upon the moral ideal and image of his own person that someone bears in his mind. To the extent that his sin reveals his incapacity to live up to this ideal, or that it involves a flagrant contradiction to this ideal, he will be thrown down from his "moral" security and will be humbled.

human passions that are not in themselves evil, but are evil only when they incite us to neglect high morally relevant values. We are thinking, for instance, of a poor man who is placed in a situation that tests his honesty because it offers a temptation to alleviate his misery by fraud or theft. Or let us imagine a man undergoing temptation because he deeply loves a divorced woman.

The temptations of which we are thinking presuppose the presence neither of vices nor of moral perversions. They refer to situations that demand a sacrifice from us either of a legitimate, subjectively satisfying good or even of an objective good for us, because in such situations its possession is possible only by disregarding a morally relevant good or by disobeying a moral commandment. The God-given meaning of temptation—often mentioned in the Holy Scriptures and in the Liturgy—is precisely a "proving" in the good. It is *this* type of temptation that the correct man may not have undergone. His general will to tread "the paths of the Lord" has never been tested because of his having a placid, comfortable life and a certain bluntness and apathy.

It is this sense of temptation that we were referring to when we said that the experience of temptation that we overcome makes us aware of our frailty and sinfulness. The attractiveness of the goods that we are not allowed to possess, or even to desire in certain situations, the very experience of this attractiveness, reminds us of our frailty and opens our eyes to the drama of morality.

The absence of grave sins does not yet guarantee the presence of moral virtues. As long as we know only that a man has never committed murder, theft, adultery, fornication, we have not yet ascertained whether he is humble or charitable, nor can we be certain of how great and deep his love of God is. Only when we know that someone has been tested, that he has undergone temptations in the abovementioned sense of the word, and that nevertheless he has abstained from sinning, may we presume the presence of positive, moral virtues.

Yet this role of temptation—always in the sense mentioned above—is restricted to the case of the mere absence of grave sins. Temptations do not have the same function when we are confronted with positive good actions and attitudes. When someone generously forgives a wrong inflicted upon him or helps a poor man, we do not need the test of temptation in order to presume the presence of positive moral attitudes. Whether or not the man had to overcome a temptation (the temptation to omit such an action) does not add a new moral significance to this action. Any difficulty the man may have had to overcome may here be only a test of the degree of his charity. But it is in no way necessary for the presence of a moral attitude. The moral rank of these actions may be increased only through sacrifice, which obviously differs radically from temptation.[10]

In analyzing the cases of the noble and of the tragic sinner we clearly saw which elements in their attitude may give them a moral superiority over the self-righteous man,[11] and even over the blunt, mediocre man who is never in flagrant nonconformity with a moral commandment merely because of lack of temptation to be so. All these elements are independent of sinning as such. Any attempt to endow sin with a certain glory, or to see in it a protection against pharisaism and self-righteousness, or to minimize the ugliness of it, is thus absolutely futile.

Yet, as we stated before, that sinning is not an antidote to self-righteousness results also from the fact that we find self-righteousness in many "sinners." There are many bourgeois types who lead an impure life and are ruthless in their attitude toward people who work for them, but who simultaneously look down with self-righteous indignation on anyone who steals or goes bankrupt. They feel themselves to be extremely decent, correct, and morally secure. Notwithstanding their grave sins, they do not have the slightest conscious-

---

[10] Cf. *Christian Ethics*, p. 387.
[11] It is, above all, because self-righteousness is a still greater moral disvalue, or a worse sin.

ness of their sinfulness. They think of their own impurity with a smile, reflecting a mixture of pride and self-indulgence. A man of this type will say, "True, I am not the epitome of virtue. I am not a virtuous youngster." The lack of charity and even of justice in his attitude toward his employees presents itself to him as a matter of course and as morally unobjectionable.

Thus we must admit not only that there are innumerable people who sin without having any humility or any consciousness of their sinfulness, but also that there are those in whom we find a typical combination of sinning and self-righteousness. It is especially the man who has replaced the true moral sphere by one substitute or another (such as honor, tradition, the laws of the state, etc.) whose conscience will not register certain actions as immoral since they are not in contradiction to his substitute. The one who makes a cult of honor would be humiliated by doing something dishonorable, for example, by stealing, breaking his word, or attacking a defenseless person from behind. Killing someone in a duel, however, or doing something impure, or being uncharitable, will not affect his conscience since it is not "dishonorable" and will thus not humiliate him.[12]

The adherents to substitutes for morality are often self-righteous and tainted with pharisaism. They abide by the letter of their substituted moral measure, a code of honor, the laws of the state in which they live, the tradition of their own society. They "judge" everyone who fails to live up to it, at the same time relishing their own "moral" superiority. They may commit horrible sins, for instance, the sins of impurity, irreverence, pride, ambition, but because these sins imply no contradiction to their moral substitutes, such persons combine a despicable moral status with pharisaic self-righteousness.

Finally we find even the paradoxical case that certain immoral persons (debauchees or unreliable and unscrupulous

[12] These substitutes will be analyzed later on in detail. Their analysis will form the main part of our next volume.

bohemians) display a feeling of moral superiority with respect to virtuous men whom they consider to be pharisees. They feel themselves to be honest, "sincere" sinners, in contrast to the "virtuous hypocrites." They regard themselves as humble individuals who do not conceal human weakness, in contrast to the self-righteous preachers of virtue. They consider themselves open-minded in contrast to the narrow-mindedness of virtuous people. They say, "We do not abide by the letter; we do not look down on sinners; we do not judge; we are aware of man's weakness." But in this attitude they themselves become self-righteous; they themselves become tainted with the pharisaism of which they unjustly accuse all virtuous men. In this defamation of virtuous men, in which their pride takes a hidden revenge, the "sincere" sinners become just as false and hypocritical as self-righteous men.

In the spiritual climate of rationalism and Rousseauism one opposed the ideal of an *"ingénu,"* unpresumptuous man, as being the prototype of unspoiled nature, to the self-righteous and even hypocritical "virtuous" man. At the opposite pole to that of the self-righteous man was not, as at the present time, the tragic sinner, but the morally unconscious type who is good-hearted, naïve, noble-minded in many respects, though committing many sins, for instance, a Tom Jones [13] or the *Ingénu*.[14] Tom Jones is presented, above all, as being antithetical to a hypocrite like Blifield, and what is stressed is his lack of self-righteousness, his mildness toward others, the fact that he does not judge them. He really is a kind of sinner who has no pharisaic trends. But he also lacks real humility. He is protected against pharisaism by his moral unconsciousness. While his naïve, unreflective attitude makes pharisaic tendencies impossible, his lack of a general will to be morally good, of a clear conscious position toward the moral sphere, and his indifference toward God also exclude true

[13] Hero of Fielding's novel, *Tom Jones*.
[14] Hero of Voltaire's novel, *L'Ingénu*.

humility and a true consciousness of his sinfulness.[15] He remains on a morally immature level and is immune to pharisaism at the cost of moral consciousness and moral maturity. Thus Fielding, Voltaire, and many others in their day also proposed an antithesis to pharisaism and self-righteousness that was fundamentally wrong.

Today, certain people worship, not the *"ingénu,"* the morally unconscious, "lovable" sinner who is unaware of his sins, but rather the tragic sinner who knows that he sins. Whereas the *"ingénu"* is presented as the product of "nature" in contradistinction to the pious man, modern sin mysticism presents the tragic sinner as the true Christian who puts all his hope in God's mercy, in contrast to virtuous men who in reality still attribute to their own justice the merit of their moral perfection.

We want to emphasize that the appeal to God's mercy is really honest and sincere only if a man has the basic will to follow the paths of the Lord, if he hates sin, and ardently strives to avoid it. Only the one whose love of God manifests itself in the firm will to abstain from sin, though living in the full consciousness that God's grace alone can hold him close to Christ, has the possibility of appealing to God's mercy, because he knows that having done what he could, he still remains an unworthy servant.[16]

It must be stressed, however, that self-righteousness is often met with even among those people who believe themselves to be the protagonists in the fight against pharisaism. The very same people indulge in an indignation resembling that of self-righteous zealots when it comes to their hatred of mediocrity. They are prone to view every thrifty person as a potential miser and are always eager to detect a lack of heroism in their neighbors.

It is very important to stress this type of self-righteousness because it is very widespread today, especially among adher-

---

[15] Cf. *Christian Ethics,* Chapter 18.

[16] St. Augustine says: "Make neither of your own righteousness a safe-conduct to heaven, nor of God's mercy a safe-conduct to sin."

ents of circumstance ethics and sin mysticism. In their fight against bourgeois mediocrity and conventionalism, they feel themselves superior. They believe they are the sincere representatives of the true Christian spirit. They do not pretend to be correct, to be without sins. No, they pride themselves on being true Christians notwithstanding their sins, because, as they say, pharisees alone care much about not sinning. They not only feel superior, but like the self-righteous zealot, they gloat over their indignation about mediocre bourgeois and self-righteous Christians. When they rage about the self-righteousness of others, it makes them feel free, great, deprived of all pettiness and mediocrity. The kind of vices they generally suspect is characteristic. Whereas the self-righteous zealot prefers to be on the scent of sins against the sixth commandment, of dishonesty, of unreliability, this revolutionary type of self-righteous man everywhere suspects avariciousness, lack of charity, mediocrity, conventionalism, hypocrisy, and insincerity.

Like the self-righteous zealot, he lives on the *qui vive* to find an object for his indignation, and like the self-righteous zealot, he makes no differentiation between an ascertained fact, in which the intention (*Gesinnung*) is laid bare, and mere appearances that might eventually be interpreted in the direction of something to be indignant about.

As with the self-righteous zealot, the slightest appearance suffices for him to make a "judgment" on other people. The mere rumor of avariciousness, of lack of charity, of mediocrity —unfounded as it may be—seems to entitle him to pass a final sentence. This type also shares hypocrisy with the self-righteous, inasmuch as, by his manner of condemning self-righteous people, he himself becomes self-righteous.

We can see to what unfortunate results the fight against pharisaism has led. Instead of opposing to self-righteousness the humility and charity of the saint, one slips into sin mysticism, a glorification of sinning. One ends by fighting the devil with Beelzebub, and by becoming pharisees of sinning.

Chapter IX

## THE CHRISTIAN ATTITUDE TOWARD SINNERS

If "judging" the sinner is a characteristic mark of self-righteousness, what attitude should the true Christian take toward his neighbor's sins? Should he completely abstain from judging? Should he never respond with indignation when witnessing an evil deed? Should he only regret it and experience sorrow, but remain silent? Certainly not. It is of the utmost importance to elaborate the truly Christian attitude toward other persons' sins as constituting a double antithesis to pharisaism and to an attitude of *"laisser vivre, laisser aller."*

Our question clearly does not refer to a judgment pronounced by Holy Church. Christ said to the Apostles:

Whatever thou shalt bind on earth shall be bound in Heaven, and whatever thou shalt loose on earth shall be loosed in heaven.[1]

The condemnation of heresies, errors, and wrong principles belongs to the very mission of Holy Church. The same is true of excommunication and the placing of a ban on individuals, whether as a public response to the unrepenting sinner or as an automatic consequence of the sinner's attitude. But it is the same Holy Church who prays every moment for the conversion of sinners, who awaits them anxiously and lovingly, in order to accept them like the father who received the prodigal son as soon as he said, "I want to return to my father's house." Holy Church reflects in her attitude the attitude of God, Who judges the living and the dead and Who, in ineffable mercy, however, elevates the repentant sinner.

[1] Matthew, 16:20.

## THE CHRISTIAN ATTITUDE TOWARD SINNERS

To see any taint or danger of pharisaism in the anathema, excommunication, or ban of the Holy Church is tantamount to a misunderstanding of the very nature and meaning of Holy Church, as well as of the nature of pharisaism.[2]

The question that occupies us here is rather the attitude of an individual Christian toward the sins of others. It is only here that the danger of pharisaism or self-righteousness may exist.

The first fundamental distinction we must make involves considering whether a "judgment" refers to the *sinning* of a person or to wrong moral *principles* expressed by a philosopher or a writer or contained in the program of a political party, in the creed of a sect, or in the constitution and laws of a state.

It is clear that a "judgment" against false principles is not a case in which the danger of pharisaism is acute. Certainly the way in which someone condemns a wrong principle may also betray a pharisaic taint. But the anathema, as such, implies no danger of slipping into a pharisaic attitude.

The delight in condemning others, in feeling oneself above them, in relishing the "hardness" of anathema, can be a mark of a pharisaic trend. The "anathema" as such, however, is morally called for. Whenever wrong and evil principles are at stake, a clear-cut repudiation is a moral duty. Not only does it not contradict the Christian spirit, but it is implied by it.

Certainly, one must not judge a principle before having taken the trouble to understand it correctly. One must not anathematize a theory because of its terminology or its merely

---

[2] A typical misunderstanding of this duty and of wrongly seeing it in the light of pharisaism is the open letter of Graham Greene addressed to the Archbishop of Paris, Cardinal Feltin.

Because Cardinal Feltin did not grant a religious funeral to the French writer Colette (she was twice married outside the Church), Graham Greene attacked the Cardinal in a way that clearly shows that he considers the attitude of the Cardinal as somewhat tainted by pharisaism. The Church's normal procedure when someone by his own free decision has severed himself from her Communion is considered by Graham Greene as a presumptuous self-righteous "judging" of another person.

apparent similarity to other morally wrong theories. But as soon as the moral evil of a principle, theory, or program is indubitably stated, a clear-cut, unequivocal rejection is obligatory, always so in *foro interno* (in private), very often also in *foro externo* (in public).

It makes no sense in this case to apply the words of Christ, "Let him who is without sin among you be the first to cast a stone." Our own moral standard has no bearing upon our right and our duty to reject evil principles. Whether we live up to what we know to be morally right or not, whether we are without sin or not, morally wrong principles must in any case be rejected.[3]

The words of St. Augustine, *"Interficere errorem, diligere errantem"* (Kill the error; love the one erring), indicate clearly what the Christian attitude should be. The person or persons who propagate wrong moral principles must be loved, but this love in no way alters the fact of the necessity of killing the error. On the contrary, it necessarily includes it.

It is important to stress that the words of our Lord, "Let him who is without sin among you be the first to cast a stone," do not apply to the definite and unequivocal anathema hurled at morally wrong principles that are propagated publicly. To hold them anathema is a strict duty and is completely consistent with the Christian spirit. It in no way contradicts humility or charity. On the contrary, the *interficere errorem* is a consequence of the *diligere errantem*. The indignation and rejection are, above all, necessary consequences of the love of God and as such imply no taint of self-righteousness. They are focused on the object, supported by truth, motivated by the love of God, and have no reference to our own ego.

The obligation to condemn false principles must be

---

[3] Hypocrisy, however, may also intervene in the condemnation of principles when one propagates similar principles himself. But this condemnation has no pharisaic character. It is an insincere condemnation accomplished with the purpose of deceiving others and of attaining some practical purposes. It includes no self-righteous satisfaction whatever. It is a purely hypocritical attitude in the sense of Tartuffe's.

stressed today not only because from time to time a pseudo-Christian attitude has been voiced in the face of systems such as Nazism or Bolshevism—thus it has been said that we have no right to condemn these systems because of our own moral faults—but also because of the widespread existence of the idol of pseudo objectivity that identifies objectivity with neutrality. Many people believe that the only objective, unprejudiced, and just approach is a kind of academic, cool distance, dealing with everything as if it were a merely interesting, peculiar problem and abstaining from any judgment in terms of true or false, right or wrong, good or evil. Accordingly they look upon any anathema as presumptuous arrogance or as merely an expression of uncontrolled emotions. This idol of pseudo objectivity, which is nothing but a consequence either of a radical skepticism or of making a fetish of science, forms a radical antithesis to Christianity and to the spirit of the Gospel. The champions of this neutrality also feel themselves in some way to be specifically antipharisaical. They consider themselves superior to the "judging," condemning spirit of the Gospel, rating themselves above the "judging," condemning people, whom they look down upon as being pharisaical.

In truth, however, they themselves are a new species of pharisee, exhibiting a self-righteousness of pseudo objectivity, a sense of superiority because of their scientific, neutral, nonaffective approach. Because of a certain hypocrisy also, they have some affinity with the pharisee. Their hypocrisy lies in the fact that, on the one hand, they have a quasi-scientific approach, with the implicit claim to objectivity and the superiority proper to true objectivity, and on the other hand, they deny real objectivity by the relativism that is at the basis of their idol of neutrality. They are in a certain way hypocrites because they put on the garments of true objectivity while in fact they deny any true objectivity. They arrogate to themselves the dignity of true objectivity and look down on prejudiced, emotional people. But simultaneously they reject the measure of objective truth that true objectivity necessarily presupposes. Since they have substituted an emasculated neutrality for true objectivity, they are hypocrites for glorifying themselves because of their scientific dignity.

Compared with them, those who because of their relativism substitute an openly subjective, arbitrary approach for an objective one are more honest and less hypocritical.[4]

Turning now to the question concerning the judgment and condemnation of sins, we have again to make further distinctions. The truly Christian attitude will vary in accordance with our having or not having any *function* that imposes on us preoccupation with and judgment of the moral life of other persons. It is obvious that a spiritual director has the duty of watching over and judging the moral life of the person who has chosen him as director. It is *his* responsibility, and here the question of his own moral standard must not influence his judgment. The words of our Lord, "Him who is without sin," do not apply in the sense that the spiritual director should not condemn a moral failure that he himself also possesses. As spiritual director, or as father confessor, he acts in accordance with his function as a representative of Christ, and not as a private individual. He would commit a grave moral fault if he took his own moral standard as the measure for judging the person whom he is directing spiritually.

The same applies to every person who has the specified function of having the moral care of other persons—such as a superior or novice master in a religious order, parents in relation to their nonadult children, or the educator, in short, any moral authority. The attitude of all these may be pharisaic or self-righteous. But they will be pharisaic, not because they blame, judge, and condemn sins or give moral advice. It will be because of their merciless, hard, pedantic way of judging. It will be because they fail to take all the motives and circumstances into consideration, because they cleave to the letter instead of the spirit. They may also be pharisaic by relishing their function of having to judge and the superior

[4] Cf. *The New Tower of Babel,* "The Dethronement of Truth."

position that it implies, instead of experiencing it rather as a cross imposed on them. They are pharisaic if they abuse the "superiority" of their function as if it were a superiority of their individual moral standard.

But this clearly results from not distinguishing the God-given function in question from the individuality of the one who exercises the function. It is the reverse of the case in which a spiritual director fails to condemn a moral fault because he possesses it himself. He confuses his individuality with his function. He rightly sees the sinfulness of his own individual person and wrongly deduces from it the impossibility of fulfilling what his function morally imposes on him to do. The self-righteous spiritual director or superior, on the contrary, confuses function and the individual person by arrogating to his person the superiority of the function and relishing this superiority as if it were his own.

The moral judgment or condemnation that someone gives by reason of his special office and function must remain secret, so long as the sin does not have a public character. It is very significant that the father confessor has to keep absolute silence about confession. In a less rigid manner, the spiritual director also has to keep secret the sins or faults of the soul guided by him. Only in cases involving a moral danger to others is he, in contradistinction to the confessor, permitted to warn them.

We stress this point because it is a specific mark of the self-righteous man not only to rejoice in the moral failures of others but also to publicize [5] them. To keep secret the

---

[5] This does not mean, however, that every disclosure of the sins of others has a pharisaic taint and results from self-righteousness. Sometimes the motive may be pure sensationalism, either in the form of a curious longing to know the *"chronique scandaleuse"* and a longing to be the first to spread it, or of the thoughtless joy of a chatterbox. This form of concupiscence clearly differs completely from pharisaism and self-righteousness. The inquisitive gossip is especially eager to spread affairs having an intimate character. He has no preference for spreading unfavorable things. Favorable or unfavorable, it does not matter to him. That things are intimate and private suffices to satisfy his sensational tendencies, especially if these things are unusual.

The gossip spreads good and evil things indifferently. However, being

moral faults of other persons instead of making them public is a clear sign of our charity, of our sorrow over our neighbor's fault, and of the absence of our taking self-righteous pleasure in them.

The desire to keep secret the moral faults of other persons, to cover them as Sem and Japheth covered their father with a coat, is a general requirement for the Christian approach toward sinners. It also applies to educators, parents, and anyone having a function implying an educational duty.

A completely different situation is given if the office in question extends to the public sphere and embraces more than persons who are either seeking advice or in one's tutelage. The prophet is also called to condemn publicly the sins of kings and official personalities. St. John the Baptist denounced publicly the sinful marriage of Herod with Herodias.

This also applies to the case of any person who in a certain situation receives the mission of making an evildoer realize his evil action or of influencing him to withdraw from an evil undertaking. It is a moral duty, with no pharisaic taint whatever attached to it, to proclaim the sin of an aggressor and to denounce his sinful intentions and activities in the process of resistance. Such was the judgment proffered by Fra Cristoforo against Don Rodrigo in Manzoni's novel *The Betrothed*. Even a person not holding a special office that imposes on him the task of giving a moral judgment of certain persons may, by the very situation in which he is placed, have to assume this function, and it would be either cowardice or *respect humain,* or even moral indifference for example, if he did not speak up and publicly denounce the moral evil of an aggressor.

After having eliminated the cases in which judging as such does not imply the danger of pharisaism (though it does not exclude pharisaical abuse), we now turn to cases in which neither aggressiveness, nor public danger, nor a specific office

eager for the sensational does not exclude pharisaism. There undoubtedly are persons who combine self-righteousness with curiosity and being a gossip.

or task imposes on us the obligation to judge others. Let us consider our attitude toward our neighbor, our attitude in the course of our everyday life when confronted with the sins of others. What should be the Christian attitude, in contradistinction to the pharisaic or the self-righteous one? Again we must distinguish, this time between the case in which we learn that someone has sinned, for example that he committed adultery, that he yielded to an impure temptation, or that he went into fraudulent bankruptcy, and the case in which we are informed about the evil mentality and immoral intention of a certain person.

In the case of a morally bad *"Gesinnung"* (an evil principle) underlying his action, for example, moral cynicism, complete moral indifference, or a *ressentiment* against the sphere of morality, I have to take a position other than when I merely hear about the moral fall of someone. If somebody sins, having an underlying immoral mentality, the Christian should not simply overlook it. He should, in *foro interno*, definitely condemn this mentality and intention as being morally evil. The case is somewhat analogous to the case of morally evil principles mentioned before. The difference is simply that whereas those principles were propagated with the claim that they were true, here the evil moral principles manifest themselves only in the actions of the person and in his incidental speech.

If we take as an example a Father Karamazov or an Iago, it is obvious that one should not ignore such immorality, and that at least a response of rejection in *foro interno* should take place. Even a merely passive sorrow and condoning (such as we find them in Alyosha [6]) is not enough. With an element of real moral horror in it, an unequivocal judgment should be pronounced upon it.

Yet this response differs radically from the judgment of the self-righteous or mediocre correct man. First, this rejection is not tainted with any satisfaction at all. Instead of the pleasure in the rejection that we find in the self-righteous

[6] Alyosha, the hero of Dostoievski's novel, *The Brothers Karamazov*.

man, we find here a deep sorrow and a sincere horror. Instead of looking down from the pedestal of one's own perfection, here one shudders, realizing the frailty and weakness of man. One feels compassion for the sinner's immortal soul.

The true Christian, instead of finding in his neighbor's evil mentality a means of throwing into relief his own moral perfection, will rather examine himself more anxiously to see how far he himself is free from similar tendencies. A neighbor's evil-mindedness is, for the self-righteous man, a ladder up which he clambers to his "perfection," whereas for the Christian it is a reminder of man's frailty and of the constant danger of his falling himself.

Starting from the basic conviction that his own moral condition would be in question if God's grace had not protected him,[7] unlike the self-righteous man, he is frightened rather than reassured by a neighbor's moral misery.

Furthermore, the Christian's rejection differs from that of the self-righteous individual insofar as the urge to make known publicly the wickedness of the sinner is absent. The true Christian will not speak about the moral wickedness of his neighbor if there is no special need to do so. But if this wicked mentality should endanger another person morally, the true Christian would obviously condemn it openly. The same applies when the situation calls for an open resistance to the evildoer's actions. But as long as there is no special reason, he would reject them only in *foro interno*. The sinner's misdeed is a real grief to him, whereas the self-righteous man rejoices over it, and thus also rejoices in making it public.

The true Christian always distinguishes the person as a whole from his evil mentality. He allows him the benefit of doubt regarding the degree of his guilt, and he hopes and prays for his conversion.[8] He combines love for the sinner

---

[7] St. Augustine says about his conversion: "...and I was able to do it, because You were my helper." *Confessions,* VII, 10.

[8] St. Augustine says: "I still hate such vicious and perverse creatures, but I love them as subjects for amendment..." *Confessions,* V, 12.

and hope for his conversion with the clear, implacable anathema of the morally evil mentality. He really desires and yearns for this conversion, whereas, when the self-righteous man prays for the sinner's conversion, an element of hypocrisy creeps in, for he does so rather for the sake of feeling himself "charitable" and to increase his sense of an "abyss" separating him from the sinner.

The true Christian always combines with his rejection of an evil mentality the consciousness that the degree of guilt of a man is a mystery known only to God and that, although we clearly see the moral horror of it, we never know how it all came to pass and under what circumstances and influences he sank to this abominable level.[9] This dimension of mystery is completely absent from the mind of the self-righteous man, whether zealot or mediocrity.

All these distinctions lead us to the very core of the difference between the Christian attitude toward other persons' evil-mindedness and the judgment of the self-righteous.

The self-righteous individual arrogates to himself in his judgment a position that is reserved to God alone. The Christian, on the contrary, is fully aware that he is neither capable of nor called to give a final sentence. He sees the evil-mindedness, he rejects it as evil, he deplores it as an offense against God. But "judging" in the full sense is more than rejecting something as evil. For to judge means to pronounce the verdict in regard to a person, to anticipate, as it were, the punishment that the sinner deserves from God. This is precisely what the self-righteous man does, and what the true Christian always avoids doing.

---

[9] St. Augustine admirably describes the unscrutableness of man's mind:
"If by abyss we understand a great depth, is not man's heart an abyss? For what is there more profound than that abyss? Men may speak, may be seen by the operations of their members, may be heard speaking; but whose thought is penetrated, whose heart is seen into? What he is inwardly engaged on, what he is inwardly capable of, what he is inwardly doing, or what purposing, what he is inwardly wishing to happen or not to happen, who shall comprehend? ... Do not you believe that there is in man a deep so profound as to be hidden even to him in whom it is?" In Ps. XLI, 13.

The true Christian rejects the evil-mindedness of his neighbor on his knees, so to speak. The self-righteous man, on the contrary, sits on a throne and pronounces his condemnation. The Christian puts the evil-mindedness of his neighbor in God's hands, and rejecting and deploring it, he confides the sinner to the divine Judge's mercy. The self-righteous man, on the contrary, anticipates God's judgment and takes it for granted that he is entitled to share in God's judgment. The true Christian's rejection is made in a spirit of charity and of humility. The self-righteous man lacks both charity and humility.

Yet if the true Christian rejects, whereas the self-righteous individual "judges," in the true Christian attitude the "no" is a real and valid one, whereas in the self-righteous individual's judgment it is in fact an invalid one, a spurious rejection.

The true Christian really opposes evil. He really is concerned with it. He rejects it because of its evilness as such. The self-righteous man opposes it ultimately for the sake of his own superiority, and instead of being really concerned with it, he relishes his own indignation. His "judgment" is not a value response, that is, a rejection of something because of its moral disvalue. The true Christian is objective. He is really interested in the object; he is concerned with it as such; his rejection is really motivated by the moral disvalue on the side of the object. The judgment of the self-righteous man, on the contrary, is hypocritical. He acts as if he were concerned with only the moral disvalue, but in fact, he is concerned with his own perfection, with the satisfaction of his pride. To say the least, the judgment of the self-righteous is always tainted with the desire to enjoy his own moral superiority. It is a mixture of value response and the satisfaction of one's own pride. But this mixture strips his rejection of the character of a true, sincere, and valid opposition to moral evil.

The rejection by the true Christian is a necessary result of his love of God. It is an organic manifestation of his love of

God, of his understanding of the incompatibility of moral disvalues with God's infinite Holiness, and of his hatred of moral evil. He cannot but reject evil-mindedness; he cannot but condemn it if he really loves God.

The true Christian's love of God necessarily entails a firm, unequivocal "no" to a morally evil mentality, as well as a deep sorrow over the offense against God. The self-righteous man has no real love of God. His "judging" is not rooted in love of God, but rather in his own moral "dignity." Much as he speaks of God and of his interest in the sinner's welfare, actually he is *not* concerned with the offense against God. This clearly discloses itself in the fact that in reality, he rather rejoices than suffers over the sinning. He rejoices because he takes pleasure in indignation and "judging" and because his neighbor's moral failure throws into relief his own moral superiority.

Thus we see that the true Christian's condemnation of the wicked mentality is a real one, precisely because it is the pure value response, and not a response mixed with self-satisfaction and pleasure in one's own superiority. It would be a great error to believe that the rejection of the moral evil, as such, is more intense and more definite in the self-righteous. That would be confusing the hardness of the condemnation uttered by self-righteous and mediocre correct men with the depth and validity of the true rejection.

The hardness of the self-righteous man is a result of his pride and is in no way a result of the intensity of his value response. The hardness is absent in the true Christian's rejection, but intensity, depth, and definiteness are much greater in him. In him the "no" given to the wicked mentality is a real and valid one; whereas the condemnation of the self-righteous man is a sham "no" and a morally invalid one. In the self-righteous man, moreover, the condemnation always remains on a conventional level, and notwithstanding its hardness, it is ultimately superficial, betraying the shallowness of a conventional ethos.

It completely lacks the **inner validity and metaphysical**

strength of the "no" that is to be found in the true Christian rejection. The scandalized raising of one's head that we find in the self-righteous man betrays clearly that he is in fact concerned with his own emotion, that he lacks any real interest in the other man's doings and rather capitalizes on them in order to relish his own moral indignation and to confirm the sense of his own moral superiority. Thus the Christian rejection, though free from all hardness, is in no way less intense and less firm than that of the self-righteous man, but it is even the only true, serious one, and, above all, the only valid one.

We can see clearly how ridiculous it is to deny that a Christian should reject the evil-mindedness of others, and how wrong it is to see every rejection as a symptom of pharisaism. In fact, the true Christian's rejection not only differs from the self-righteous man's judgment, but is even its very antithesis.

The rejection of others' evil-mindedness to which the Christian is committed is a result of his love of God and his love of neighbor. It is formed by charity and imbued with humility. It is an act endowed with a specific moral value. It is even obligatory. The self-righteous judgment is rooted neither in the love of God nor in the love of neighbor. It is an outgrowth of pride and is definitely tainted with hypocrisy. It is an act endowed with a great moral disvalue.

The words of our Lord, "Do not judge, that you may not be judged," patently do not refer to the rejection of evil mentalities, in which immoral principles have become a lived reality. It refers, first of all, to "judging" in the sense of a final sentence, such as that which the self-righteous man pronounces. It refers to arrogating to oneself the position of a judge in the sense in which it belongs to God alone. It refers further to evil done to us, to injuries inflicted on us, that we should forgive, and to the mercy that we should show when our right to blame a person who has wronged us places us, as it were, in a morally superior position toward him.

The attitude of the Christian differs in the most drastic

way from the "judgment" of the self-righteous, however, when he is confronted with the single sins of his neighbor. Someone hears that a man has committed adultery, that he has stolen, that he has committed perjury, or that he is guilty of some fraudulent transaction. It is here that the antithesis between the self-righteous man, zealot or mediocrity, and the true Christian is most striking.

To begin with, the Christian will *never* judge before knowing the motives, the inner attitude that the sinner himself has toward his sin, and before knowing all the circumstances. He will always give the sinner the benefit of the most favorable interpretation of his fall, so long as he is not forced to accept the unfavorable one. Certainly, he knows that in any case, something morally wrong has taken place when there is a nonconformity with a moral commandment that includes an absolute veto. But in regretting this moral evil, he will strictly abstain from "judging" the *man* in any sense of the term. He will not yet form an opinion of the action's *specific* moral quality,[10] of the degree of the man's responsibility, and still less of the man's character.

The self-righteous man, on the contrary, will precisely feel entitled to a full judgment as soon as he hears of the man's objective sin.

Moreover, even when he knows for a fact what the whole story is, the Christian will abstain from judging, fully aware that he is not called upon to render judgment on the weakness of his neighbor. The words of our Lord, "Let him who is without sin among you be the first to cast a stone," apply precisely to the case in which we are confronted with the fall of another. Fully aware of our own weakness and misery, of the constant danger of falling, we should, seeing another fall, deplore it, but beat our own breast and pray for him. The way in which inwardly we should turn to the sinner is the very opposite of having the feeling of being protected in the fortress of our own moral superiority. The Christian does not condescendingly manifest a compassion that is only an

[10] Cf. Introduction, pp. 8–9.

elevation of oneself above the sinner. In no way does he close his eyes to the moral evil of the sin. Far from remaining indifferent, as if nothing had happened, he deeply regrets the sin, and he is shaken by it. He deplores the offense against God that has taken place and the evil that the sinner has inflicted on himself by sinning, but he does not identify the sinner with his sin. In an attitude of true charity he turns to the sinner without reference to his fall. The Christian is fully aware of the responsibility on his side. First, he never knows whether the other would perhaps not have fallen had he himself been as he should have been. Secondly, he realizes that lack of charity toward the sinner may push him farther away from God. The Christian feels that he himself may be responsible by having perhaps acted as a screen barring the light of God and making it invisible to the sinner. And he knows that now, after the fall of his neighbor, he himself may become not only an obstacle to the sinner's rising, but even a means of pushing him deeper into misery.

The difference between the Christian attitude and that of the self-righteous man is clear. Again, it is not simply a difference, but an antithesis. Yet the Christian attitude is never an antithesis to self-righteousness because of indifference toward other persons' sinning. In the Christian attitude we find no effacement of the clear frontiers of sin and nonsin and no blotting out of moral commandments. Nor is there any viewing of the moral sphere as though it were in a state of constant flux.

Instead of being blunted before the drama of good and evil, the Christian sees this drama in its full grandeur and seriousness. His attitude is in another way an antithesis to that of the self-righteous man inasmuch as he sees in its complete metaphysical grandeur the abyss separating good and evil; whereas the self-righteous man, whether zealot or mediocrity, ignores the metaphysical grandeur of this abyss and its intimations of eternity. The indignation of the self-righteous man manifests what seems to be merely the shock of witnessing nonconformity to convention.

The words of Saint Augustine admirably express the true Christian attitude toward sinners:

> ... not to hate the man for his vice, nor to love the vice for the man, but hate the vice and love the man; for the vice being cured, he shall find no object of his hate, but all for his love.[11]

[11] *The City of God,* XIV, 6 (Healey, *op. cit.,* p. 32).

Chapter X

# BASIC ERRORS OF CIRCUMSTANCE ETHICS

WE MENTIONED in the introduction that there are great differences among the adherents of circumstance ethics. Some of them go much further than others. In this chapter we intend to concentrate on the most extreme theses of circumstance ethics, theses in which a rebellion against the very nature of morality comes to the fore. We shall ignore to a great extent sin mysticism, with which we have already dealt.

First of all, circumstance ethics tries to eliminate from the moral sphere the elements of commandment, obligation, and oughtness. The champions of circumstance ethics would do away with every bond. Because of their idol of freedom, they interpret the intrinsic "oughtness" character of the moral sphere as being an adaptation of morality to the juridical sphere.[1]

Justified as is the reaction against viewing morality in a merely juridical light, against "legalism," the attempt to oust "oughtness" and obligation from the sphere of morality is nevertheless fatal. The attempt to escape from the yoke of morality, from its intrinsic oughtness, is ultimately an escape from the *servire Deo,* even though it is disguised in the religious formula of filial relation between the "I" of our person and the "I" of God.

In every value there is a mysterious oughtness. Every good endowed with a value not only simply exists, but is also "should be." We have dealt with this ultimate character of the important-in-itself in *Christian Ethics.*[2] We also stressed that this element assumes a new character in the moral values.

[1] Cf. Introduction, p. 7, and Chapter V, "Freedom of Spirit."
[2] Cf. *Christian Ethics,* Chapter 18.

Now we want to emphasize this difference. It is indeed a completely new oughtness, superior to the oughtness of other values not only in degree but also in essence. Having in mind the ultimate seriousness and the central character of the moral theme, the unique relation of moral values to God, we cannot but grasp that the oughtness of moral values has still another character than the oughtness of other values. The moral sphere is linked to the *unum necessarium* not only in the sense of the one important thing for man, but also in the sense of the one important thing in itself.

This mark of the moral sphere reveals itself above all in the challenge addressed to us by morally relevant goods. We saw in *Christian Ethics* [3] that an adequate response is due to every good endowed with a value. But to the morally relevant good, a response is due in a new sense. The "due-ness" here assumes an incomparable character. This difference in "dueness" is strikingly obvious when a moral obligation is at stake.

Yet the difference in the oughtness of the response is in no way restricted to the cases in which the call of the morally relevant good has an obligatory character. We want to stress here an element that is proper to the entire moral sphere, and that is present in the call of every morally relevant good, always and in any case, although it finds its most typical expression in the moral obligation.

If, understanding the moral significance of a morally relevant good, one accomplishes a morally good action, one *also* necessarily grasps this "oughtness" even if no obligation is at stake.

The general will to be morally good that is at the basis of a morally good action, the obligatory as well as the non-obligatory, is indissolubly linked with an awareness that the morally good action should be accomplished, in a sense which clearly surpasses the oughtness of all extramoral value responses. Every moral value response implies an element of obedience that corresponds to the specific oughtness of the

[3] Cf. *Christian Ethics*, Chapter 18.

moral sphere, of the morally relevant goods. Yet in order to grasp the unique oughtness proper to the moral sphere, we have to consider another antithesis that will also lay bare the very core of the error of circumstance ethics.

Sometimes one contrasts the man who, without struggle and in a superabundantly loving attitude, does what is morally right, with the man who submits with his will to the moral law, who obeys it *à contre coeur*. One interprets the former as acting morally well, not because he should do so, but because he loves to act so. Freed from any imposition from without, not obeying, but acting spontaneously, this man seems to be endowed with the freedom of the children of God.[4]

This antithesis is not concerned with the difference between an obligatory good moral action and a nonobligatory good moral action, but with a difference in man's approach, which is to be found in the case of moral obligation as well as in the case in which there is no moral obligation.

In truth, however, this interpretation of the freedom of the children of God is wrong. Two different things are tacitly being identified: the character of spontaneous superabundance of an affective moral value response, and the absence of any awareness of an oughtness.

It is true we may distinguish two types of morally good actions. The one is accomplished with an iron will, struggling against the tendencies of our nature, and the other is joyfully accomplished without struggle, with the ease that has often been stressed as characteristic of virtue.

Yet in both cases, the element of a unique moral oughtness is to be found. The difference between them in no way lies in the fact that in the former alone is there an awareness of oughtness, while in the latter the action is accomplished without any consciousness that it should be done. The decisive error here consists precisely in identifying the spontaneity of the superabundant, joyful moral value response

---

[4] Cf. Introduction.

with the spontaneity of a response to a morally irrelevant good, for instance, the enthusiasm for a work of art.[5]

It may suffice to stress that this unique oughtness is also to be found in the most spontaneous affective value response, for instance, in the burning love of neighbor found in the saints or in a mystic's most ardent love of God, responses to which the Augustinian *"parum voluntate, etiam voluptate"* [6] applies.

This is clearly shown by the way in which every moral act is sanctioned by the morally conscious man. Whereas we can give a *"nihil obstat"* with our free spiritual center to all kinds of attitudes, granted that they are morally unobjectionable, that is, to instincts, responses to merely subjectively satisfying goods, responses to objective goods for the person, as well as responses to morally irrelevant values, *moral value responses alone* can be sanctioned in the full sense of the word.

This superabundant love, full of bliss and delight, is sanctioned by our free spiritual center, not in the sense of a mere *"nihil obstat,"* but in the full, real sense that is possible only when one is confronted with morally relevant values.[7] This sanction is deeply embedded in the awareness of the unique challenge of the morally relevant good and of the oughtness of the morally good act. It is essentially connected with the formal characteristic of the moral sphere and of the moral theme, namely, the intrinsic element of oughtness that distinguishes the moral values from all other values.

This element implies that every morally good act, even when it is a superabundant value response arising spontaneously with delight and bliss, is nonetheless experienced as something that *should be* and that it contains an element of obedience. Certainly, in this case, it will be a blissful obedience, and not the rigid obedience that has to struggle to over-

---

[5] In a later publication, we shall analyze in detail the decisive difference between the moral value response and all other value responses in respect of the character of "oughtness."
[6] St. Augustine, *Tractatus 26 in Joannem.*
[7] Cf. *Christian Ethics,* Chapter 25.

come the resistance of our nature, of our desire, and even of our heart, but nevertheless an element of obedience, of *"religio,"* that is, of the bond to God. Thus the desire to liberate ourselves from this weight, to replace morality, with its oughtness and majestic obligation, by a spontaneous value response that has the same character as enthusiasm for a great work of art, is at bottom an attempt to elude the moral sphere.

Three grave errors are to be found in this attempt, which is disguised in the garment of the "freedom of the children of God."

First, there is the misinterpretation of the meaning of the freedom of the children of God. Instead of opposing the spontaneous value response of love and the "being drawn by delight" to the aridity of obedience *à contre coeur,* one interprets this spontaneous value response in a manner that would strip it of its specific moral character. One ignores the free sanctioning of this response with its specific awareness of the moral oughtness. One places it on the same level with our extramoral value responses or even our likings.

Second, one deals with the case of arid obedience, of a submission to the moral law *à contre coeur,* as if this were a wrong kind of morality. In a certain way, this is to commit an error analogous to that of Kant. Circumstance ethics, like Kant, identifies the blissful moral value response with a mere inclination in which we follow our likings. Both overlook the authentic nature of the blissful spontaneous moral value response. They differ only in the evaluation of this "spontaneous" response. Kant erroneously refuses any moral value to the blissful value response, let us say, of loving, and considers only the case of arid obedience, of "duty," as morally good. Here, on the contrary, one praises the spontaneous moral value response because one has falsely identified it with an extramoral value response.

In reality these two forms of moral response are two different stages of one and the same morality. And if we certainly will admit that the joyful and blissful moral value response, in which the heart also participates, ranks, as such, still higher, it is absolutely wrong to separate both as though from the moral point of view they were antithetical, and to deal with arid obedience as something that does not deserve full praise. Both are parts of the one true morality, and arid obedience also deserves the full title of a truly good act.

Third, one forgets that arid obedience is, in general, the way leading to that kind of obedience we have called blissful. So much do they belong together that the former is normally the only way to attain the latter. One assumes naïvely that at least every true Christian has already attained the stage of this blissful freedom of the children of God. One forgets that being drawn by delight to the morally good and responding spontaneously with a blissful love to morally relevant goods is either a privilege that may be granted to us as a specific gift in certain rare moments, or a stage of religious development that presupposes for many persons the long hard road of arid obedience. Thus, instead of being antithetical to "being drawn by delight," arid obedience, is, under normal circumstances, the *only* way leading to a blissful response.

A unique oughtness is an essential feature of morality; obedience is an essential element of every true moral value response. Every attempt to do away with this oughtness and to efface the decisive difference between the moral value response and any other value response is tantamount to a radical misinterpretation of morality.

Another basic error of circumstance ethics derives from the attempted elimination of general principles of morality. It declares every moral decision to be based on a unique situation and to be the result of a confrontation of the "I" of the person with the "I" of God.

In order to unmask the grave error that is here in question, we have to disentangle different elements that are tied together.

The fact that circumstances vary on every occasion and that, besides the awareness of the general morally relevant values, we have to discover their specific modification in each individual case, far from throwing into opposition the role of the general morally relevant values, necessarily presupposes it. If we have to decide in an individual case—let us say in a totalitarian state—whether or not we are justified in taking a false oath because we are put under pressure, we obviously must bear in mind the general moral character of an oath, the moral disvalue of perjury, as well as the intrinsic presuppositions for an authentic oath, in order to decide what we shall do. We have to grasp that the pressure may undermine the authentic nature of an oath, and thus, deprived of its authentic moral substance, this false oath would not constitute a perjury.

True as it is that the individual concretization of a general value, principle, or commandment is an important process of its own and a decisive element of the greatest importance in our moral life, it is wrong to believe that the concretization in an individual and perhaps unique case invalidates the general character of the morally relevant or of the moral values, or of the moral commandments. The decisive grasping of our God-given task in the single case presupposes essentially the knowledge of general moral values, of general moral commandments or laws. For example, in order to know that I should risk my life in one case and that I am morally not allowed to do so in another, I have to know, first, as something general, that I have no right to dispose of my life according to my own arbitrary mood. Second, I must know which goods justify the risking of my life—such as, for example, saving another person's life—and which goods even oblige me to sacrifice my life—for instance, in a situation in which the alternative were to sin. If we have to dispense with all moral principles and commandments, with all moral values and disvalues that are connected, as such, with certain actions and attitudes, if we have to ignore all the morally relevant values of different goods, the decision of our conscience in the confrontation with God would be impossible. The single occasion would provide no knowledge as a basis for what I should do, except in the case of a commandment addressed by a private revelation by God, as was the case with Abraham, a case so extraordinary that it can certainly not be assumed as a basis for our moral life.

Saying that every decision of our conscience already requires the knowledge of morally relevant values, we do not imply, however, that this knowledge must necessarily precede the concrete individual situation that calls for a decision. It may just as well be that we discover a morally relevant value for the first time in a concrete situation. But our decision is possible only after this morally relevant value has been perceived. And this value is by its very nature something general, transcending in its validity, the concrete situation. Let us take a case of conversion, such as that described in the life of Staretz Zossima in the *Brothers Karamazov* of Dostoievski. The young, thoughtless, and superficial officer brutally slaps his groom in the face because of some trifling matter. Afterward, his servant's face, with its silent and submissive expression, keeps rising before his mind, accusing and tormenting him. All at once, he discovers the nobility of a human being and the horrible disvalue of his brutality. Here he grasps in a concrete situation, and for the first time, a morally relevant value and a moral value. Yet here it is not only the moral disvalue of his own action in this concrete case that is grasped, but the general, moral disvalue of brutality and the general value and dignity of a human person are also perceived. This discovery is the starting point of Staretz Zossima's conversion.

This objection to the thesis of circumstance ethics does not mean that all moral decisions are based on a tacit syllogism applying a general law to a single case. This would indeed be a very incorrect interpretation of conscience and of the way in which moral decisions are made.

When a juridical law is in question, a tacit syllogism may be a correct interpretation of applying the general law to a concrete case. But we saw before [8] that we must distinguish moral commandments from purely legal ones and, further-

[8] Cf. Chapter V, "Freedom of Spirit."

more, in the frame of morality, formal obligations from material ones. In the latter cases, the application requires more than a syllogism.

Above all, there are many cases in which the application of fundamental moral commandments, for example, to love thy neighbor as thyself, requires the perception of the morally relevant values at stake in a concrete situation. The process of understanding what morally relevant values are at stake in a concrete situation (values that are as such general) is not a mere syllogism. It implies an intuitive concrete value perception.

What we object to is the denial of the role of general morally relevant and moral values, as well as of general principles and laws, rooted partly in these morally relevant values, partly in positive commandments of God.

In this context it seems indispensable to analyze briefly the notion of conscience, which plays such a predominant role in circumstance ethics.

> We do not intend to offer a complete analysis of one of the most important moral data: conscience. Admirable things have been said about conscience by many great Christian authors and a thorough analysis of this great, mysterious voice in man would require a book of its own. Here we shall only attempt to unmask the equivocal use of this term in circumstance ethics.
>
> We shall begin by quoting Cardinal Newman, who characterizes the nature of conscience in an admirable way:
>
>> What is the main guide of the soul, given to the whole race of Adam outside the true fold of Christ as well as within it, given from the first dawn of reason, given to it in spite of that grievous penalty of ignorance, which is one of the chief miseries of our fallen state? . . .
>> I do not say that its particular injunctions are always clear, or that they are always consistent with each other, but what I am insisting on here is this, that it *commands*,—that it praises, it blames, it promises, it threatens, it implies a future, and it

witnesses the unseen. It is more than a man's own self. The man himself has not power over it, or only with extreme difficulty; he did not make it, he cannot destroy it. He may silence it in particular cases or directions, he may distort its enunciations but he cannot, or it is quite the exception if he can, he cannot emancipate himself from it. He can disobey it, he may refuse to use it; but it remains.[9]

Notwithstanding the mysterious grandeur of conscience that Cardinal Newman points out, as well as the role of moral guidance that it plays, we must stress that conscience is *not* the organ with which we grasp morally relevant or moral values. The goodness of justice, the evil of injustice, the intrinsic beauty of purity, the horror of impurity are perceived and understood by something other than conscience.

The value of a human person, the sacredness of man's life, the dignity of truth are not grasped by conscience. Conscience presupposes the knowledge of these values. It is not through conscience that we discover moral values, morally relevant values, and divine commandments.

The predominantly negative character of conscience already points to this fact. Socrates stressed that conscience rather warns us not to do morally evil things than commands us to do morally good things.[10] Socrates perhaps went too far in his statement, but he certainly touched upon a very typical and characteristic feature of conscience. Though conscience also intervenes in a positive direction, it is certainly true that warning against going morally astray is in a way its foremost function.

Something else that reveals that conscience is not the organ of moral value perception is the fact that the voice of conscience refers exclusively to our own doings and not to those of others. But moral value or disvalue is discernible in the actions of other persons also, and perhaps even more

---

[9] Cardinal Newman, *A Newman Synthesis,* arranged by Erich Przywara (New York: Sheed & Ward, 1945); quoted from sermons preached on various occasions, London, 1857.
[10] Plato, *Apology.*

clearly than in our own. Conscience thus refers only to our own moral life. We are said to have a bad conscience because of our own moral failures and not because of other persons' sins. No one will claim that our conscience is involved when we grasp the sublime charity of a saint, are deeply moved by it, and respond to it with joy, enthusiasm, and veneration.

Conscience, moreover, always acts with reference to concrete situations, whereas our moral value perception refers as well to general principles as to concrete situations. All these features clearly show that conscience is not the organ through which we grasp morally relevant and moral values.

At the same time, they show how impossible it is to sever conscience from the perception of morally relevant and moral values and from the reference to moral commandments. In reality every prompting of conscience refers to moral commandments and morally relevant and moral values. It therefore necessarily presupposes the knowledge of them.

The function of conscience is to warn us in a concrete situation not to yield to morally evil tendencies or to sinful passions by inviting us to turn to the morally good, to "the path of the Lord." "Conscience" is, at it were, the *advocatus Dei* in our soul. It presents to our mind the impact of morality, of guilt and merit. It calls imperatively in the direction of the good; but it does not by itself tell us that it is good. It presupposes the knowledge of moral values and moral commandments. But it is the mouthpiece of the morally good, ultimately of God, and its precise function displays itself in the very clash between the temptation of the subjectively satisfying and the call of morally relevant values. It places the obligatory character of the moral commandments before our mind, but it presupposes the knowledge of these commandments.

It is impossible to oppose the voice of conscience to the knowledge of general values and commandments, saying: "I follow only the voice of my conscience and do not care about general moral principles." The voice of conscience always implies precisely a reference to general moral principles. The only question is whether the general moral principles presupposed are the true commandments, either revealed or implied by the moral law, or whether those principles have been adapted to our subjective mood and arbitrarily distorted. The question is whether our value perception is adequate, whether we grasp the real morally relevant and moral values, or whether pride and concupiscence have affected this value perception and produced a condition of moral value blindness.[11] The man who is morally value blind will do evil actions without having a bad conscience. As soon as a moral disvalue is in question, a moral disvalue to which he is blind, conscience will fail to warn him. Many people commit impure actions without any intervention of their conscience. Others practice birth control or social injustice without any pangs of conscience. To maintain that therefore they do not sin is completely wrong, for they are generally responsible for their value blindness. To say it suffices to follow our conscience, declaring that for God the only thing that counts is a good intention, is a radical moral subjectivism and formalism.

Value blindness, especially in the form of substitutes for morality,[12] may, however, not only silence our conscience with respect to various immoral attitudes, but may also make our conscience intervene in the wrong way. The man for whom "honor" replaces morality may be directed by his conscience to fight in a duel, although duelling is morally wrong.

The Corsican, Matteo Falconi,[13] feels himself compelled

[11] It is impossible to enter into a detailed analysis of value blindness. Here it suffices to stress that moral value blindness is not a lack of a natural disposition, such as, for example, a sense for music or art, but in most cases (if not a mere fruit of tradition) it is a result of pride and concupiscence for which one is responsible. Cf. *Christian Ethics* and *Sittlichkeit und ethische Werterkenntniss* (Halle: M. Niemeyer, 1921).
[12] Cf. Chapter VIII, "Sin Mysticism."
[13] Hero of Prosper Mérimée's novel, *Matteo Falconi*.

by his conscience to shoot his own son. Value blindness or morally wrong traditions may lead to an intervention of conscience in a morally evil direction. Conscience may then prompt us to do what is morally wrong.

The special function and nature of conscience comes to the fore also if we realize that the wicked man, that is, the enemy of God, has, as it were, no conscience, or rather, that in principle he does not care about the voice of conscience. His basically antimoral attitude manifests itself precisely in the fact that he has turned his back on the *advocatus Dei* in his soul.

These hints alone should suffice to show that a "voice of conscience" that would act without any value perception and knowledge of moral principles does not exist. A conscience that is not supported by value perception or by knowledge of moral principles is blind and mute. What matters, however, is whether our conscience is supported by an adequate value perception and guided by the true moral commandments, or whether it relies on value blindness or is guided by wrong moral principles. The true voice of conscience looks for guidance. The true Christian attitude implies a full awareness of all the possible deceptions of our conscience and of the necessity to look for guidance to the divine commandments:

> ... in spite of all this Voice does for them, it does not do enough, as they most keenly and sorrowfully feel. They find it most difficult to separate what it really says taken by itself, from what their own passion or pride, self-love or self-will, mingles with it. Many is the time when they cannot tell how much that true inward Guide commands, and how much comes from a mere earthly source. So that the gift of conscience raises a desire for what it does not itself fully supply. It inspires in them the idea of authoritative guidance, of a divine law; and the desire of possessing it in its fulness, not in mere fragmentary portions or indirect suggestion.[14]

---

[14] *A Newman Synthesis*, p. 25.

Nobody will deny that to live in the presence of God and to confront every live concrete situation with Christ is the expression of the highest Christian life.

But it makes no sense whatsoever to oppose this confrontation to the general moral and morally relevant values or to general moral principles and general moral commandments.

This confrontation, on the contrary, presupposes in various directions the knowledge of moral and of morally relevant values, which by their very nature are general, as well as the knowledge of general moral principles and commandments.

This confrontation may have a manifold character. It may be that the concrete situation is difficult and complex, one in which different goods are in conflict. The confrontation with Christ then has the very function of helping us to perceive the morally relevant values at stake in their authentic nature. In the light of Christ we hope to be freed from all subjective illusions and to be able to grasp all values at stake in their objective and true light. In the confrontation with Christ we also hope to receive from Him the strength to act according to His spirit and His commandments.

In such confrontation, general values, principles, and commandments clearly play an indispensable role. This confrontation with Christ implies the awareness of the infinite holiness of Christ, of the wealth of supernatural values embodied in His Sacred Humanity. Indeed, it is only in this light that the question of whether something stands the test before Him assumes a real meaning at all. Yet all these values have precisely the character of something generally good, good in any case, absolutely good.

Moreover, in this confrontation we aim at grasping what is morally right in a given situation and thus compatible and in conformity with the spirit of Christ, i.e., we aim at grasping clearly the morally relevant values in question, or how the commandments of Christ apply. The confrontation with Christ is thus so far from replacing the knowledge of morally relevant values or the moral law rooted in them, or of the general commandments of Christ, that it is precisely through this confrontation that we hope to understand the moral significance of a situation.[15]

When the moral significance at stake is obvious, such as, above all, an obligation to abstain from sin, for example, from cursing or fornication, the confrontation with Christ does not have the function of enabling us to understand what is morally right and thus according to His spirit and will. Our confrontation with Christ here has the meaning first, of putting on the armor of light in order to withstand better all temptations and overcome our weakness; second, it has the function of making our resistance to evil an outgrowth of our love of Christ. But in no way does it serve to enable me to find out whether or not I may be allowed or even obliged to do sinful things in these special circumstances. The very expectation that a confrontation with Christ could have such an outcome is clearly nonsensical. There is no need for examining whether or not I should act so.

Yet the confrontation with Christ may also have the specific meaning of discovering whether or not something is the right thing for *me* to do, given my individual vulnerability, even if it is objectively something morally unobjectionable or even morally good. Here the uniqueness of the individual

---

[15] It is certainly true that there are many situations in which we cannot simply deduce from concrete moral commandments what we are called upon to do morally speaking. It often occurs that no commandment of the Decalogue applies to the specific situation. For example, we have to finish an important work that is due on a certain date. We have a strict formal obligation to postpone other things. But a person in distress wants to speak to us. He wants advice from us. What should we do? Certainly no commandments exist that could simply be applied, but we have to grasp the morally relevant values at stake, in order to find out which of both conflicting obligations is more important in God's eyes. We must take into account all factors, consult all the relevant values in question. We mentioned in Chapter V those cases in which the call of God speaks to us through morally relevant values without the help of formulated concrete moral commandments. Here we must rely on our value perception. But values are general and thus in this case also the indispensable role of general principles clearly manifests itself.

case assumes a specifically personal character. The question is raised of whether or not, for my individuality, it would be right to do a certain thing—whether it is in accordance with the will of God.

It is probably *this* uniqueness that is the starting point for circumstance ethics. Its champions argue that the general commandments and principles cannot answer the question of what *I* should do in a given concrete situation.

It is true, to a certain extent, that general commandments and principles *alone* cannot always yield an answer. Yet, this in no way means that general commandments and principles are invalidated.

The question—whether it is for *me* the right thing to do to act in this particular way—only arises when morally unobjectionable or morally good things are at stake; but never when indisputably immoral things are in question. If someone proposes something impure or something sacrilegious to us, there is no sense in posing the question of whether or not it is precisely for *me* the thing to do. The answer is that in any case, every person—whatever his individuality may be—should abstain from doing something indubitably immoral.

Thus this question arises only if something morally unobjectionable (for instance, whether or not I should accept a position) is for *me* without moral danger, whether or not it may expose a nature such as mine to temptations of pride or concupiscence. Or it arises when we are confronted with doing something morally good. Should I intervene in saving another person in moral danger? Should I give someone a good and objectively right admonition? Here it may be that it would be the right thing for another person to do, but not for me. Given, let us say, a tendency to dominate other people, to govern them, the role of a moral adviser would be morally dangerous for us.

Only our confrontation with Christ can answer this question. Only in the light of Christ is a real self-knowledge possible.[16] Only in the light of Christ can we see ourselves as we are in reality. In the full surrender to Christ, in the disposition of our will to do whatever Christ wishes us to do according to His will, we may hope to advance the distance toward our real selves and to be able to see that a certain thing that as such is good may not be the right thing for us to do.

It is especially illustrative for grasping the basic error of circumstance ethics—the expelling of general moral principles and commandments in the name of the individual unique call of God addressed to me—to see that, precisely in this question of the will of God for *me,* moral values, general moral principles, and commandments are necessarily presupposed.

We have first to perceive whether the action in question is, as such, morally good or evil. If it is something universally and by its nature morally evil, the question of whether or not I should do it is already answered, because I definitely should never do it—neither I nor any other person.

Thus the comprehension of moral values and of general moral commandments rooted in them is already presupposed in order to decide whether this question as such can arise.

Moreover, in aiming at a real self-knowledge, that is, at an understanding of whether as a result of my individual character moral dangers are in question if I perform a certain action, I again refer to general principles. I have to grasp the relation between this good action and my pride or concupiscence. Although it is as an individual that I am especially exposed to these dangers, the relation between such a type of action and pride or concupiscence is not only an

---

[16] Cf. *Transformation in Christ,* Chapter III.

Strictly speaking, this question can be answered at best through spiritual direction. It is easier to have this distance to one's wishes, self-illusions, and self-deception, when we advise another person than when we examine it for ourselves. The great function of spiritual direction and moral authority here comes to the fore. But in case we have no occasion to consult a spiritual director, and even in the application of his advice, we shall find an answer through this confrontation only.

individual one, but it is rooted in the action on the one hand and in pride and concupiscence on the other. Without grasping this general relation, I could never reach a decision in one individual case.

Finally, in this case, as in any confrontation with Christ, I have to grasp the infinite holiness of Christ, the wealth of the supernatural virtues of His Sacred Humanity. I have to know His commandments, all of them—commandments that surpass all individual cases and remain unchangeable and absolutely valid, whatever individual person and whatever circumstances may be at stake.

Yet the confrontation with Christ may also have a completely different function. It may be that it serves to enable us to find out what the will of God is in a situation in which a moral problem is at stake neither on the object side nor on the subject side. We refer here to something that is, as such, beyond the moral sphere and that makes sense only on the basis of a deep religious life. In the framework of natural morality, man is certainly permitted to choose according to his inclination if no moral problem is involved, that is, if there is no moral obligation on the object side and none deriving from his individual nature. He may, for instance, choose the profession that attracts him most, granted that no moral danger is involved.

But the *homo religiosus,* who conceives his life as guided by the loving plans of God, who understands that he is morally bound to conform to these plans, even if in their substance they do not refer to moral questions, has the task of finding out, in every extramoral decision, what the will of God is for him—the unique, individual plan. We find innumerable examples of such questioning in the life of saints.

It would clearly be ludicrous to take this case, which, as such, lies beyond the specifically moral life, as the pattern of our moral conduct. The function of this type of confrontation with God appears precisely when all moral obligations, direct and indirect, are absent. To declare this case to be the only norm for our conduct is equivalent to behaving as if there was no morality at all. Moreover, in this case also, the moral values, the moral principles, and commandments are not really ousted.

In order to know whether or not a situation is morally relevant in itself, I have to refer to the morally relevant values and to moral commandments. I must refer further to the general principle that I should conform my life to God's plans. Thus, as we can easily see, the attempt to expel the general character of morality is completely futile. It is a complete distortion of the real uniqueness of the application in the individual case in whose name this attempt is made.

The argument that the uniqueness of the individual case is incompatible with general principles is so far from being true that even in the rare case of an absolute uniqueness, for instance, the sacrifice of Abraham, the moral value of his attitude is general, and we can say, "Everyone who might be in Abraham's situation should act likewise."

Circumstance ethics implies a certain form of moral relativism. It is a more refined relativism, which does not declare that the notions of morally good and evil are merely subjective. It reduces the notions of good and evil neither to mere feelings nor to fictions. Yet the validity of general moral commandments and principles is denied. This amounts to denying that certain attitudes are good as such; for instance, that love of neighbor is morally good intrinsically, whether here in this world or in any other possible world. It would further deny the obvious fact that certain attitudes *are* morally evil, such as adultery, fraud, treason, murder, fornication, and blasphemy.

If matters were as circumstance ethics claims, no moral pattern would exist, no moral education. If every decision were morally good only for one individual case, if there were no general values invested in this individual situation, no virtuous person could ever—because of his virtues—become a moral example. There would be no influence by example and no moral education besides the one that prescribes making every decision in a confrontation of my conscience with God, without any other data. We have mentioned already that this would be tantamount to restricting all morality to the positive commandments of God and to presupposing that God would reveal such a commandment to us as soon as we consult Him in our conscience. There would, above all, be no imitation of Christ, that is, no full abandonment to Christ, which implies the knowledge of the overwhelming divine wealth of virtues in His Sacred Humanity and all the moral values embodied in His infinite Holiness. The imitation of Christ presupposes not only this grasping of moral values, but our being imbued with them. It implies that every step in our life is under the yoke of His commandments, and it includes a confrontation of the morally relevant values in every concrete situation with the Spirit of Christ.

Paradoxically enough, circumstance ethics leads, through an absolute formalism, to a much more radical "legalism" than the one against which it protested. It arose originally as a protest against an undue "legalization" of morality, against a disregard of the qualitative plenitude of morality. Yet in denying the existence of general morally relevant and moral values, as well as the existence of moral commandments and moral laws rooted in these values, in effacing the difference between a moral commandment and a mere positive commandment, it leaves no other beacon for our moral life than a private revelation of God's will, referring exclusively to a concrete, unique situation. The only norm left would be orders that we have to follow blindfolded, instead of commandments that reveal to our mind that something is evil or that something is good.

Circumstance ethics is, moreover, a radical ethical formalism, perhaps still more radical than the Kantian ethics.

Though not denying the objective validity of the notions of good and evil, circumstance ethics excludes the possibility of determining what is morally good or evil, because, according to this theory, what is good and evil changes in every individual case and depends upon factors that cannot repeat themselves. The morally good is what our conscience tells us to do in a unique case when we examine all factors before God.

It is obvious that such a formalism opens the door to a complete subjectivism. There would exist as many different types of good and evil actions as there are individual cases. This theory also ignores the great danger of value blindness and the craftiness of our nature, which darkens our conscience almost *ad libitum* when deprived of any norms, principles, and general moral values.[17]

The qualitative unity of the moral sphere would be denied. Morality is then reduced to an ever changing qualitative content, the unity of which exists exclusively in the formal feature of being a dictate of our conscience before God. This conception of morality bears the seal of an artificial construction. Experience reveals to us the very existence of qualitative moral values, such as generosity, purity, humility, meekness. Experience reveals unequivocally that certain attitudes are morally good essentially, for instance, charity, and others essentially evil, such as envy or hatred. The denial of the fact

[17] The aversion to moral laws, principles, and commandments that characterizes circumstance ethics testifies, as already mentioned, as much to a great presumption as to an unrealistic, naïve illusionism. It overlooks the incalculable benefit that the moral law, moral principles, and commandments embody, in helping our weakness, in protecting us against the enormous, continuous danger of self-delusion and self-deception. He who is aware of the weakness of our fallen nature, he who understands the enormous role of moral value blindness, cannot but see how lost we would be if we were to rely exclusively on our individual value perceptions, and were to be deprived of the firm, unshakable, unalterable principles of the moral law.

The fact that the natural moral law is objectively rooted in the moral and morally relevant values, in no way guarantees that our conscience would lead us according to these values without the knowledge of the natural law. Sometimes, this delusion is a result of a theological error, namely, the idea that through the redemption of Christ, we are cured from the frailty that exposes us to value blindness and self-deception. The adherents of this error reason that as redeemed men, we no longer need commandments, principles, and laws. The spirit of Christ will lead us. But this is just the opposite of what our Lord tells us: He who loves me will keep my commandments. The entire Gospel is pervaded by a warning against self-deception, and nowhere is the promise given that after baptism we are no longer exposed to the snares of Satan. St. Peter addresses his warning, *"Fratres sobrii estote,"* to Christians.

that these attitudes as such essentially possess a definite value is in glaring contradiction to experience.[18]

Moreover, it is especially absurd to claim that the absence of general principles is a specific mark of Christian morality. In reality, there are general commandments in Christian as well as in natural morality, and in both we have the task of an ever new application in the individual case with all its circumstances. Not only does the Decalogue, which coincides in many parts with the natural moral law, include general commandments, but the two commandments of Christ, love of God and love of neighbor, also bear a general character. Both the natural moral law and the commandments of Christ require that our conscience find in every concrete individual situation those attitudes that are the application of general principles and the concrete individual outgrowth and consequence of their general spirit.

In both natural and Christian morality, there exist attitudes that are, as such, morally good; there exist goods that have a morally relevant value, as well as responses to them that are objectively and essentially endowed with moral values. The presence of morally relevant values and moral values having a definite essence and a general validity is an indisputable reality in both.

A third fundamental error is the wrong conception of the

[18] In saying "experience" we do not mean observations and inductions, i.e., experience in the sense of science. We mean the immediate contact with intelligible, evident data, which being offers to our mind, in our lived, prephilosophical communion with reality. To hypothesis or theoretical explanations, or to induction and deduction, we oppose experience as the intuition of the "given" (in the sense that we gave to this term in the "Prolegomena" of *Christian Ethics*). It is this intelligible voice of being, the intelligible data granted in our contact with being, which is also the very object of philosophy. The question whether a philosopher sees and understands them or whether he overlooks and ignores them is the measure that decides whether his philosophy is true or not, or what his philosophy is worth.
Experience in this sense excludes in no way the *veritas aeterna* or the a priori truth, the absolutely certain insight in strictly necessary states of facts. On the contrary, these insights are based on experience in this sense. Cf. *Zum Sinn des Philosophischen Fragens und Erkennens* (Bonn: Peter Hanstein Verlag, 1950), and *Christian Ethics*, "Prolegomena."

relation between natural moral law and Christian morality, the morality of the Gospel. As we pointed out in *Christian Ethics,* Christian morality represents something completely new and incomparably superior to natural morality, but it is simultaneously the ultimate fulfillment of all natural morality.[19] Now we have to stress that Christian morality in no way *invalidates* the natural moral law. It surpasses it infinitely. However, to surpass the natural moral law can in no way be equated with rendering the natural moral law obsolete.

Our Lord says that the entire law and all the prophets depend upon His two commandments. He does not say that His two commandments invalidate the laws and the prophets. Far from it, for He says that He is come "not to destroy, but to fulfill."

Circumstance ethics assumes that Christian morality invalidates the natural moral law. According to its adherents, it no longer matters whether the natural moral law prohibits something—i.e., whether an attitude is stained by a natural moral disvalue—if only it is accomplished in conformity with the filial relation between man and God. This "new" ethics presumes that an action or attitude stained with natural moral disvalue, for instance, an impure action, remaining what it is, could yet become morally unobjectionable in Christian morality.

This conception deals with the natural moral law as if it were a positive law. It forgets that the natural moral law is founded on the moral values and that the moral values and disvalues are rooted in the very nature of certain attitudes. The idea that injustice, impurity, unfaithfulness could ever become morally unobjectionable is thus completely erroneous. One forgets that the natural moral values also reflect God in a unique way, that natural moral disvalues are an offense against God and are incompatible with Him.[20]

[19] Cf. *Christian Ethics,* p. 459.
[20] The position that denies this betrays a complete disregard of the nature of the moral sphere. In characterizing moral values in *Christian Ethics,* we

The relation between Christian morality and natural morality is, on the contrary, such that the former, while surpassing the latter, includes all the natural values and excludes all the natural disvalues.

However, it may be that something that is morally unobjectionable in the framework of natural morality is not compatible with the *similitudo Dei,* because holiness is incomparably higher and exacts much more than the natural moral law. But never can a natural moral value become merely unobjectionable in Christian morality, and still less can a moral disvalue become morally unobjectionable in the light of Christ.[21]

Sometimes circumstance ethics fails to distinguish the natural moral law from certain norms that in fact are mere substitutes for true morality. We are thinking of such norms

stressed the unique and intimate connection existing between the natural moral sphere and the sphere of religion and the *similitudo Dei.* Every natural moral disvalue is incompatible with the *similitudo Dei.* Only someone insensitive to the import of natural moral values and disvalues, to their very nature, can claim that natural moral disvalues could be neutralized and become morally unobjectionable.

[21] There are certainly exceptional cases in which a specific call of God invites us to do something that would be morally evil if we would do it without this specific call. Such cases are, for instance, St. Francis's attitude toward his father, or St. Jeanne Françoise de Chantal's stepping over her son in order to go to the monastery when he threw himself before her to bar the way; or the case of St. John of God leaving his parents at the age of seven. In all these cases, the same action would be morally wrong, if there was no special call of God. This is, however, no argument for an invalidation of the natural moral law through the supernatural order. The rule that thoroughly changes an action in introducing a completely new factor, a higher value, the one embodied in the call of God, is the same that we encounter *mutatis mutandis* in natural morality. To abandon a friend is, as such, morally evil. But if this friend endangers my moral development, I must leave him. It is the general rule that when a good with higher value enters into the picture, our moral obligation changes, in other words, we are obliged to prefer the higher good to the lower one. (In what sense this obligation has to be understood has been discussed in detail in *Christian Ethics,* Chapter 28.) But on that account my obligation to respect the morally relevant value of the lower good is in no way invalidated, as long as its call is not superseded by the call of a higher value. The same applies here. Also in Christian morality it would be morally evil to abandon one's child or one's parents, if there were no special call of God that changed the situation.

as honor, tradition, *"bien pensant,"* and many others. The natural moral law is not invalidated by Christ, but rather all those norms that are illegitimate substitutes for the natural moral law.

Certainly, Christian morality is, above all, the revelation of an incomparably higher morality, the supernatural morality that surpasses infinitely the natural moral law. Yet the true natural moral law retains its full validity, even if moral values have been revealed to us in Christ that incomparably surpass the highest natural moral values.

Volume III of *Christian Ethics* will deal *in extenso* with the different substitutes for morality and analyze the nature of those distortions and perversions of the natural moral law that we find so often in the morality of various communities and individuals.

CHAPTER XI

## CHRISTIAN MORALITY

We stated in the introduction that one of our main purposes in this book is to continue to elaborate the nature of Christian morality. As a result of our critical analysis of both circumstance ethics and sin mysticism, we are now in a position to consider some new facets of Christian morality in addition to those already elaborated in the last chapter of our book, *Christian Ethics,* and to deepen and enrich our previous analysis.

We want to stress anew, and most emphatically, the radically different aspect that all of morality assumes as soon as it is seen in its relation to a living God. It is true that a man who does not know God can perceive certain morally relevant values, and that he may even give them a true value response. But as long as morally relevant and moral values are not seen in their relation to the Absolute Person of God, as long as moral evil is not understood in its character of an offense against God, as long as we ignore the fact that in the entire moral life we are confronted with God, the Absolute Judge, the full impact of morality, its ultimate seriousness, its character of being a "breath of the eternal" are absent.

Morality presupposes God objectively. We established this in *Christian Ethics.* But here we want to stress the tremendous difference that exists between the morality of a Christian and the morality that may be embodied in a man without knowledge of God and without, therefore, an awareness of the objective fact that morality presupposes God. We are not thinking here of the impossibility for fallen man of keeping the moral commandments without the help of grace, a fact known by faith alone. We are referring to the different aspects that the morally relevant values assume as soon as their relation to God is known explicitly, and of the difference in the very nature of the value response as soon as the relation of morally relevant values to God is grasped.

The splendor and metaphysical reality of morality flashes forth only when the absolute *goodness* is seen not merely as the platonic idea, but as the living God, only when it has the ultimate reality that a personal God alone possesses.

The call of the morally relevant values assumes an incomparable import, a completely new reality and rhythm, as soon as it is grasped as the voice of the living God, as soon as the entire moral life implies a confrontation with the absolute, ineffable Holy God.

The full seriousness and grandeur of morality, the fact that it breaks through the confines of this world, is divined only as a presentiment, as long as religion is vague (as it was, for example, in the case of Socrates), but it is fully grasped only in the light of a personal God. And here again a complete awareness requires us to see that morality is rooted not only in the God of the philosophers but in the God of Abraham, Isaac, and Jacob, in the God of Jesus Christ.

But even the morally relevant values, such as the value of the human person, the sacredness of human life, the grandeur and depth of the bond of marriage, all assume a new qualitative character when understood in their relation to God and when seen in the light of God. What an abyss yawns between the dignity of man as conceived in a merely humanitarian sense and man looked upon as the image of God; between a being whose personal character is only faintly grasped and a person as thought of with an immortal soul destined to an eternal communion with God. How dim is the dignity of man viewed in a merely intrahuman world, exuding a merely social atmosphere, as compared with the preciousness and nobility of man of whom the Psalmist says:

*Paulo minus sub angelis constituisti eum.*

(A little less than the angels hast Thou made him.)

Again, one can scarcely overlook the difference between the sacredness of human life apprehended in the light of God and a merely humanitarian inviolability of human life. What mystery surrounds a man's life, which is directly connected with God by the fact that every human soul is directly created by Him. Human life shares in this mysterious dignity of the soul because the soul is the very principle of man's life, even of his bodily life. And what sacredness our life assumes by the fact that we receive it from God, in order to prepare ourselves for our eternal destination, by the fact, too, that our eternal fate depends upon whether "we live according to God or according to the flesh" [1] while on earth. How shallow it sounds when unbelievers speak of the sacredness of human life, inasmuch as this sacredness is desubstantialized as soon as human life is no longer the property of God, Who, as the Lord of life and death, alone can dispose of it.

We would be going beyond the scope of our present topic if we were to trace this difference between the two moralities back through all the fundamental morally relevant values. These two examples may suffice to indicate the direction of this difference.

We can easily see the radically new character of morality rooted in the personal, living God of Revelation. Yet it is not only radically new, but this morality is also the fulfillment of all morality. The very character of morality, as such, imperatively calls for this fulfillment, and every true feature of morality finds its complete unfolding in Christian morality alone. The data of guilt, conscience, and obligation reveal themselves in their full impact, reality, and metaphysical breath here alone.[2]

Realizing all this, we cannot but note the tremendous difference of climate between Christian morality and merely

[1] St. Augustine, *The City of God,* XIV, 1.

[2] We must, however, stress that the difference between a morality without knowledge of God and Christian morality does not imply that there exists any antithesis between the true natural moral law, disclosed to our mind by the morally relevant values and Christian morality. We shall come back to this point at the end of this chapter.

natural morality. Turning from merely natural morality to Christian morality, it is as if we had come out of a dimly lighted cave into the open, filled with light and vaulted by the boundless sky.

The unique character of Christian morality discloses itself further and in a specific way in the nature of the two commandments of Christ, love of God and love of neighbor. We stated in *Christian Ethics* that one of the main marks of Christian morality is the fact that the love of God, the highest of all value responses, is simultaneously the very basis of all morality:

> ...the backbone of all moral attitudes is the love of God, through Christ, with Christ, and in Christ. The most sublime of all value responses is here the basis of all value responses; every response to a morally relevant good is rooted in this love and has the character of organically issuing from this love.[3]

Here we want to stress the unique character of the two commandments of love of God and love of neighbor insofar as they refer not merely to actions, but to the very substance of morality. The possibility of failing to conform to the spirit of morality in spite of being in conformity with the letter no longer exists here. The two commandments of Christ refer to the basic attitude that is the very core of all moral goodness.

Three things must here be thrown into relief. First, these two commandments directly refer to the very qualitative goodness of an attitude. Whenever the love of God and a love of neighbor that is organically rooted in the love of God are really present, full moral goodness is guaranteed. Unlike other commandments, which refer to actions, such as the fifth or the sixth commandment in the Decalogue, or the commandment of almsgiving, these two commandments exclude the possibility that one could conform to them, abiding by the letter alone.

[3] *Christian Ethics*, p. 462.

Second, the love of God and the love of neighbor are to such an extent the very *soul* of morality that they implicitly include the whole of morality.

Third, notwithstanding the all-embracing character of these two commandments, they are in no way merely formal [4] as Kantian ethics is. On the contrary, they point directly to the basic moral value in its qualitative plenitude. Kantian ethics restricts itself to a merely general formal principle such as, that the will should conform to reason or that the will should be *autonomous,* that it should follow what duty imposes on one, or that we should act in a way that the principles of our action could become a universal law. Any objective value or standard that might motivate our will would render it heteronomous according to Kant. Kant refuses to name any morally relevant goods. He thereby fails to indicate any moral value. He limits ethics to stating a merely formal, subjective feature, which as such does not yet guarantee a qualitative moral value, because it is cut off from the values on the object side, because the will loses its response character, and, finally, because there is no norm protecting man from a subjective distortion of morality. The same applies, *mutatis mutandis,* to the adherents of circumstance ethics, who claim that before God the objective nature of our actions does not count but only a "sincere intention." In Chapter VII we have already pointed out the equivocal meaning of the term "intention." We saw that a "sincere intention" when detached from the world of objective values is a morally void notion that leads to a radical subjectivism and formalism.

The two all-embracing commandments of Christ are, on the contrary, the very opposite of any formalism. They pre-

---

[4] The terms "formal" and "material" are here used in another sense than in Chapter V when we distinguished formal and material moral obligations. Formal is here equivalent to abstract and general, material to concrete plenitude. Formal ethics is thus an ethics that restricts itself to completely abstract principles, such as the commandment that one should do the morally good, but without saying what is morally good. In this sense Max Scheler opposed to Kant's formal ethics a material ethics of values.

scribe the full qualitative core of morality, and, far from severing the intention of the subject from the value on the object side, they refer to the basic absolute value response, that is, the response to God's infinite goodness and holiness and the response to the ontological value of every man as an image of God. They do not substitute for the commandments referring to concrete actions. Still less do they invalidate them. They have, on the contrary, a necessary and intrinsic relation to all morally relevant goods. The love of God requires imperatively a respect for all the commandments of God and for the natural moral law. It necessarily implies an adequate response to all morally relevant goods in our habitual and actual attitudes, as well as in our actions. On the one hand, every moral commandment shows us the path that God wants us to follow and which is the path truly consistent with our love of God; on the other hand, obedience to those commandments is a test of the genuine and true character of our love of God. The one who really loves God, far from believing that he no longer needs the commandments referring to actions, far from thinking, "If I love God, it does not matter what I do," on the contrary, will be eager to consult the commandments of God and those of His Holy Church in all details, and will always orientate himself anew to those commandments. He will be eager to understand more and more all morally relevant values, which precisely imply a call of God, and he will love the commandments of the God whom he loves above all.

We stressed in *Christian Ethics* that moral values, even natural ones, are a specific reflection and irradiation of God, of the God who is Justice Itself, Purity Itself, Veracity Itself, Faithfulness Itself. All human virtues are only a faint participation in God's infinite goodness. Every moral value is a natural revelation of God's nature. And, in an incomparably higher way, all the specifically Christian virtues, such as charity, meekness, and mercifulness, are a revelation of God's nature. The love of God necessarily implies the love of all natural and supernatural moral goodness. It likewise implies a horror of all moral evil, all sinfulness, which is incompatible with God's ineffable Holiness and an antithesis of it.

The same applies analogously to the commandments of the natural moral law and, *a fortiori,* to all revealed commandments of God. In them, also, God reveals Himself. They are filled with the spirit of God. Through them and in them God speaks to us. He who loves God cannot but love His commandments also. Certainly they reveal God's infinite majesty. They fill us with awe, and confronted with them, we feel the sting in our nature and sometimes even its revolt. Certainly man feels that the moral commandments are *imposed* on him, but it is the loving hand of God that imposes them, the hand of Him Whom we lovingly adore and adoringly love.

The one who loves God realizes that in obeying, in accepting the imposition of His law, he is receiving a "manna," that he is being granted a unique and blissful communion with God. Thus the true Christian, far from believing that his love of God makes superfluous all commandments referring to actions and to our positions with relation to single morally relevant goods, will hear in all the commandments the voice of God and will open himself to them, eager to know them, to delve into them, since their very content helps him to know God better, and in them he also encounters and finds the God Whom he loves.

As do all heresies and errors, the errors of circumstance ethics serve to throw certain features of Christian morality into relief. The legitimate protest made against a juridically formalized approach on the one hand, and the disastrous error of a morality relying exclusively on the voice of a subjective conscience and on the sincerity of intention on the other, help us indirectly to understand the specific character of Christian morality.

The two commandments upon which "depend the whole law and the Prophets" are the very antithesis of any reduction of morality to the juridical sphere. They prescribed the complete substance of morality, leaving no place for a mere abiding by the letter, and simultaneously they are in a necessary and organic relation to all morally relevant goods and to all moral commandments. They lay bare the mysterious relation of all morally relevant goods to the ineffably Holy God. And thereby all moral value responses assume a new splendor and sublime value. St. Augustine expresses this admirably in these words:

> As to virtue leading us to a happy life, I hold virtue to be nothing else than perfect love of God. For the fourfold division of virtue, I regard as taken from four forms of love. For these four virtues (would that all felt their influence in their minds as they have their names in their mouths), I should have no hesitation in defining them; that temperance is love giving itself entirely to that which is loved; fortitude is love readily bearing all things for the sake of the loved object; justice is love serving only the loved object, and therefore ruling rightly; prudence is love distinguishing with sagacity between what hinders it and what helps it. The object of this love is not anything, but only God, the chief good, the highest wisdom, the perfect harmony. So we may express the definition thus: that temperance is love keeping itself entire and incorrupt for God; fortitude is love bearing everything readily for the sake of God; justice is love serving God only, and therefore ruling well all else, as subject to man; prudence is love making a right distinction between what helps it towards God and what might hinder it.[5]

Above all, it is in *moral* values themselves that the difference between natural and Christian morality discloses itself. We have seen in *Christian Ethics,* first, that every morally good action assumes a radically different quality and an incomparable value as soon as it is motivated by the love of Christ. And this applies also to the sphere of virtues, for example, to the difference between the justice of a noble pagan and the justice of St. Ambrose, or between the veracity of a Socrates and of a St. Peter.

Second, we saw that many virtues are possible only as a

---

[5] St. Augustine, *The Morals of the Catholic Church,* quoted from *Basic Writings of St. Augustine,* translated by R. Stothert (New York: Random House) Chapter XV, pp. 331-32.

response to God in Christ and through Christ, and in a world seen in the light of Christian revelation, such virtues, for instance, as humility, meekness, purity,[6] charity.

Our analysis of the pharisee and of the self-righteous man in the present book has thrown into relief the all-embracing role and overwhelming impact of humility in Christian morality. It is not only the highest virtue, apart from charity, but it is, in a unique way, the precondition for all other virtues, if they are to be pleasing to God. It is the virtue that gives to all other virtues their real depth and beauty, their specifically Christian splendor. We fail to understand the true role and impact of humility if we see it as one virtue among others, such as justice, or reliability, even when we admit its superiority in rank. Humility is far more than this. It is a virtue that pervades all other virtues and makes them true. It alone opens the door to the wealth of Christian morality.

Humility provides the space in which charity can unfold itself. We have shown in other books [7] why humility is possible only as a response to the revelation of the Old and the New Testaments, especially the latter. We have shown that it necessarily presupposes a confrontation with the personal living God from Whom we receive everything and Who is Himself infinite Charity.

Here we want to stress the radical change that takes place in all morality, in every moral action, moral attitude, and virtue, through the presence of humility. This change, far from invalidating the moral value of all the actions, attitudes, and virtues that we find in natural morality, implies a fuller and purer unfolding of these values and a transfiguration of them. Humility conveys to all morality the breath of a victorious freedom and of glorious truth. Yet humility is not the indispensable presupposition for the possession of natural moral virtues. In order to exist in a person, veracity, justice, honesty, and other natural virtues presuppose necessarily a

[6] Cf. *In Defense of Purity*.
[7] Cf. *Transformation in Christ*.

basic value-responding will; but they do not necessarily presuppose humility. Without humility, they cannot, however, unfold their true beauty, sublimity, and splendor. Without humility they have still a certain poison in them, which corrodes their real value and hinders their being pleasing to God.

In this connection, we must distinguish three stages. The first stage is represented by the "honest man" who relishes his own moral goodness in a self-righteous way. Here pride undermines the moral value entirely. It turns virtues such as justice, veracity, and so on, into "brilliant vices." The second stage is that of the honest, reliable, just man, who does not glorify himself because of his morality, but who nevertheless still lacks humility. He possesses real moral values, but they lack the splendor, the transfigured sublimity, the breathtaking grandeur of Christian virtues. At the third stage, the virtues blossom on the soil of humility. It is only here that all of the other virtues, justice, veracity, reliability, modesty, faithfulness, receive a completely new character and an incomparably higher beauty and intrinsic goodness. Comparing the moral personality of Socrates and that of St. Augustine or St. Francis of Assisi, what strikes us is not merely the presence of humility in the saints and the absence of it in Socrates.[8] It is also not only the fact that in the saint we find many virtues, such as purity and meekness, which are impossible outside the Christian realm. But what strikes us most of all is the tremendous role humility plays in the entire morality of the saint, the mystery of humility, which is expressed in the words of Christ: *"Qui se humiliat, exaltabitur."* [9] (He who humbles himself shall be exalted.)

---

[8] In speaking of humility we mean incomparably more than modesty or than the absence of vanity, ambition, or any aggressive pride. Socrates certainly was modest and much too objective to be vain or ambitious. He also was filled with a great and deep reverence. But true humility, the spirit that we find in a St. Francis of Assisi rejoicing about humiliations, or that is manifested in the words of Christ, *"Non veni ministrari, sed ministrare,"* is a virtue unknown and inaccessible to a noble pagan. That the Pope—the highest authority on earth—calls himself *"servus servorum"* is unintelligible to a pagan.

[9] Luke, 18:14.

Closely related to this mark of Christian morality is the breath of mercy that pervades the entire Christian moral life. It is not a matter of a mere moral law, an impersonal moral order, which imposes moral obligations on us. It is not even a question of a personal God Who reveals Himself only as the absolute Lord and Lawgiver and Who imposes moral obligations, but it is the personal God Who opens the fathomless abyss of His Mercy. We have spoken before of the tremendous difference concerning the metaphysical impact and the full reality of morality that results from our knowledge of the existence of a personal God. But we must stress another difference. It is the fact that this Absolute Person loves us and even comes down to be among us, a fact that was "foolishness" to the Greeks, who, at best, could conceive of man's love for God, but not of God's love for us.

What we now envisage is the mystery of a dialogue between the creature and the Creator, the *mutual* situation between man and the world of values, which is now no longer a mere "world," but precisely the personal, Absolute Goodness. This implies that the "hardness" of a merely natural moral order is softened and transfigured into the goodness of the moral law itself in its relation to us—this same moral law leading us along the path to beatitude. Yet because of this, the moral law not only does not lose its majestic character, but rather assumes, simultaneously, an incomparably higher majesty:

O God Who dost chiefly manifest thy power in forbearance and mercy multiply upon us thy pity....[10]

The mercifulness of the Absolute Judge, of the ineffably Holy Lord, enlightens the entire cosmos and penetrates in a specific way the realm in which the moral life of man displays itself. It gives wings to the one who—conscious of all his frailty—strives to tread the path of the Lord. It fills with hope the repentant sinner. It permits him to say, with the

---

[10] Collect, tenth Sunday after Pentecost.

Prophet Joel, "Who knoweth but He will return and forgive." [11]

The darkness of the unchangeable reality of guilt, resulting from the impossibility of cleansing oneself from it and being freed from its crushing weight, is suddenly dispersed by the light of hope. The hardness of a merely natural moral order that is in some way analogous to the hardness in the Greek idea of fate (ἀνάγκη) is melted by the liberating breath of mercy.

This liberating breath of mercy also manifests itself in that precedence given charity with respect to all formal obligations that we mentioned in Chapter V. The words spoken of St. Mary Magdalen pervade the entire Christian morality: *"quoniam dilexit multum"* (because she has loved much). Yet true Christian humility implies also a readiness to take every small formal obligation more seriously. And the spirit of holy obedience that permeates the true Christian life gives to every task—formal as it may be—another significance.

Thus not only do the walls crumble that enclose moral obligations in the framework of formal liabilities or any other extramoral bonds, but the very formal obligations themselves are transfigured by the love of God and stripped by charity of any merely "legalistic" aspect. Every corner of the Christian moral life is pervaded by the rhythm of sacred solemnity and the breath of mercy.

We emphasized in *Christian Ethics* that the *coincidentia oppositorum* is a specific mark of Christian morality. The very fact that God is simultaneously the *Rex tremendae majestatis* and the *Fons Pietatis qui salvandos, salvas gratis*,[12] transforms the whole of morality. On the one hand, not an iota of the obligations and bonds imposed by the natural moral law is erased, and the strictness of moral obligation is incomparably increased. The majesty of moral obligation, its real impact, the terrible abyss of guilt, are revealed, as we

---

[11] 2:12.
[12] Thomas de Celano, sequence, *Dies Irae,* Office of the Requiem Mass.

saw before. On the other hand, all morality is irradiated by a new redeeming light—the mystery of infinite mercy.

Mercifulness is one of the central Christian virtues. It is even the very measure according to which we shall find mercy in the eyes of God. The completely new rhythm of this morality, through which wafts the breath of divine mercy, manifests itself also in the predominant role it gives to contrition, in which we break through to true freedom, contrition in which we "become true," contrition, this glorious resurrection in falling as a naked beggar into the loving arms of God.

In the ethics of Socrates, contrition does not play a predominant role, nor in Plato, and still less in Aristotle. In Christian morality, on the contrary, contrition holds a central position. The awareness of one's sinfulness, of the mysterious rupture in our nature, which we know by revelation to be the result of original sin, but which, as such, reveals itself also to our mind and reason, the fact that we must hope for God's mercy and not His Justice, gives to contrition a completely new role in morality. Contrition is the very core of every conversion, of every beginning of a true moral life.

Contrition, through God's mercy, not only opens to the sinner the path leading to holiness. It is not only that in a sinner that disarms us in regard to him and that endows even the greatest sinner with an irresistible beauty. It is not only the attitude regarding which our Lord says: "... there will be joy in heaven over one sinner who repents, more than over ninety-nine just who have no need of repentance." [13] It is also an indispensable element in the moral and religious life of all the saints, in a St. John the Evangelist, as well as in a St. Peter, in a St. Rose of Lima as well in a St. Augustine. The awakening to ultimate reality, the surrender of the fortress of pride, all these elements of contrition are constantly living in the soul of the saint. He finds good reason for contrition, in spite of his holiness, because his eyes perceive spots where we would no longer see them, and he measures his responsibility and guilt by the graces received from God

[13] Luke, 15:7.

and by the abyss still separating him from His infinite Holiness.

The breath of divine mercy that is wafted to us in all Christian morality also deeply changes the attitude of the Christian toward the sinner. We have dealt with this fact in the previous chapter. Here we only want to insist on this sublime quality of the Christian ethos, which distinguishes it so greatly from all natural morality. Instead of the moderate, just attitude of a noble pagan toward a morally evil person, we find in the saint a deep inner concern about the sinner, an ardent desire to win him for the good, and a love for him that is ready for any sacrifice for the sinner's conversion. It is again the marvelous sight of the *coincidentia oppositorum*. On the one hand, the sins of other persons are incomparably of more concern to the true Christian than to any pagan or humanitarian. He deeply worries about the offense against God. We see St. Francis of Assisi shed tears because "love is not enough loved." But on the other hand, in hating sin, he loves the sinner. And precisely because of his love for the sinner, he worries about his sinning, being fully aware that sin is also the greatest misfortune for the sinner. He runs after the sinner in order to win him back for Christ:

> And by that I shall see whether you love God, the Lord and me, this and your servant, if your attitude is such that nowhere in the world a brother may be found who sinned and grave as his sin may be, ever may leave you after having seen your face without finding your mercy if he seeks mercy. And if he should not ask for mercy, you should beg him to ask for it. And if he should then still sin before your eyes a thousand times, love him more than me, in order to draw him to the Lord and always have mercy of such.[14]

In Christian morality moral evil manifests itself in its full impact. Moral commandments are disclosed in their unchangeable absoluteness. The Divine Judge confers a new majesty on the whole of morality and on the immense serious-

---

[14] St. Francis of Assisi, *Letter to a Provincial.*

ness of moral obligation. But at the same time we find the breath of redemption, the mysterious liberation, the melting of all "hardness" by the fire of charity.

There is no greater misunderstanding of Christian morality than to see it in the light of a primarily prohibitive morality, a morality in which abstaining from sin is stressed more than positive moral virtues and holiness. Far more than the impact of sin is the splendor and beauty of transfigured moral goodness stressed, far more the impact of the moral virtues and their significance.

We have already dealt with the matter of the priority of abstention from morally evil actions over positive moral actions, which is proper to natural as well as to Christian morality, and which is rooted in an objective order. But this priority does not mean that abstention from sin is the more important part of morality, that it ranks higher than embodying moral values. On the contrary, in Christian morality the great theme is the overwhelming impact and importance of Christian moral values, the glorification of God by the fruits of the Holy Ghost, the splendor and beauty of purity, meekness, humility, charity, the wealth of virtues in Christ. The great theme is *holiness*.

It is deeply characteristic of this morality that the two commandments of Christ that embrace the whole of morality are positive, as well as all the beatitudes.

Closely connected with the positive character of Christian morality is also the fact that in it all moral values are grasped, not only in their majestic importance, but also in their intrinsic beauty and lovableness. In Christian morality all morally relevant and moral values also become *delectabilia;* they enchant our heart and draw us with the cords of love.

In later publications, continuing with a detailed elaboration of Christian morality, we shall insist on this most important feature. In Christ, the mysterious, inner aspect of morality, its sublime beauty and heart-melting lovableness, is revealed to us, whereas, in natural morality the outer aspect, its majestic obligation, and its character of "importance-in-itself" prevail. To express it in traditional terms, in Christian morality the delectable character of the *bona honesta* is disclosed.

Here let us at least attest to the unique interpenetration of love and obedience that is the result of the revelation of the inner aspect of morality that appeals to our love. But to this inner aspect, the outer aspect is indissolubly linked. They are two facets of one and the same reality. We saw in Chapter X that the delectability of the moral values never takes away from them their mysterious "oughtness" and incomparable majesty. The yoke of Christ remains a yoke, but it is sweet. In Christian morality obedience and love are wedded:

> Yet, doubtless He draws us "by cords of Adam," and what are those cords, but, as the prophet speaks in the same verse, "the cords" of the "twine of love?" It is the manifestation of the glory of God in the Face of Jesus Christ; it is that view of the attributes and perfections of Almighty God, it is the beauty of His sanctity, the sweetness of His mercy, the brightness of His heaven, the majesty of His law, the harmony of His providences....[15]

[15] Cardinal Newman, *Discourses for Mixed Congregations*, p. 69.

# APPENDIX

## ALLOCUTION DU ST. PÈRE À LA FÉDÉRATION MONDIALE DES JEUNESSES FÉMININES CATHOLIQUES

Soyez les bienvenues, chères filles de la Fédération Mondiale des Jeunesses Féminines Catholiques. Nous vous saluons avec le même plaisir, la même joie et la même affection, avec lesquelles il y a cinq ans Nous vous avons reçues à Castel-Gandolfo à l'occasion de la grande rencontre internationale des Femmes Catholiques.

Les impulsions et les conseils de sagesses que vous a donnés ce Congrès, comme les paroles que Nous vous avons alors adressées (Discorsi e Radiomessaggi, IX, pag. 221-233) ne sont vraiment pas restés sans fruit. Nous savons combien dans cet intervalle votre effort s'est tendu, pour réaliser les buts précis, dont vous aviez la claire vision. C'est ce que Nous prouve aussi le mémoire imprimé que vous Nous avez remis lors de la préparation du Congrès d'aujourd'hui: "La Foi des Jeunes— Problème de notre temps." Ses 32 pages ont le poids d'un gros volume, et Nous en avons pris connaissance avec grande attention, car il résume et synthétise les enseignements d'enquêtes nombreuses et variées sur l'état de la Foi dans la jeunesse catholique d'Europe, et le résultat en est extrêmement instructif.

Toute une série de questions qui y sont touchées, Nous les avons Nous même traitées dans notre Allocution du 11 septembre 1947, à laquelle vous assistiez, et dans beaucoup d'autres Allocutions auparavant et depuis. Aujourd'hui Nous voudrions prendre occasion de cette réunion avec vous, pour dire ce que Nous pensons de certain phénomène qui se manifeste un peu partout, dans la vie de foi des catholiques, qui atteint un peu tout le monde, mais particulièrement la jeunesse et ses éducateurs, et dont votre mémoire aussi rapporte en divers endroits les traces, ainsi, quand vous dites (pag. 10): "Confondant le christianisme avec un code de préceptes et d'interdictions, les Jeunes ont le sentiment d'étouffer dans ce climat de 'morale impérative' et ce n'est pas une infime minorité, qui jette par dessus bord 'le bagage gênant.' "

*Une Nouvelle Conception de la Loi Morale.*

Nous pourrions nommer ce phénomène "une nouvelle conception de la vie morale," puisqu'il s'agit d'une tendance qui se manifeste dans le domaine de la moralité. Or c'est sur les vérités de foi que se basent les principes de la moralité; et vous savez bien de quelle importance fondamentale il est pour la conservation et le développement de la foi, que la conscience du jeune homme et de la jeune fille soit très tôt formée et se développe selon des normes morales justes et saines. Ainsi la "nouvelle conception de la moralité chrétienne" touche-t-elle très directement au Problème de la foi des Jeunes.

Nous avons déjà parlé de la "nouvelle morale" dans Notre Message Radiodiffusé du 23 mars dernier aux Educateurs Chrétiens. Ce que Nous disons aujourd'hui n'est pas seulement une continuation de ce que Nous avons traité alors; Nous voulons dévoiler les sources profondes de cette conception. On pourrait qualifier celle-ci d' "existentialisme éthique," d' "actualisme éthique," d' individualisme éthique," entendus au sens restrictif que Nous allons dire, et tels qu'on les trouve dans ce qu'on a appelé ailleurs "Situationsethik," morale de situation.

*La Morale de Situation. Son Signe Distinctif.*

Le signe distinctif de cette morale est qu'elle ne se base point en effet sur les lois morales universelles, comme par exemple les Dix Commandments, mais sur les conditions ou circonstances réelles et concrètes dans lesquelles on doit agir, et selon lesquelles la conscience individuelle a à juger et à choisir. Cet état de choses est unique et vaut une seule fois pour toute action humaine. C'est pourquoi la décision de la conscience, affirment les tenants de cette éthique, ne peut être commandée par les idées, les principes et les lois universelles.

La foi chrétienne base ses exigences morales sur la connaissance des vérités essentielles et de leurs relations; ainsi fait St. Paul dans l'Epitre aux Romains (1, 19-21) pour la religion comme telle, soit chrétienne, soit antérieure au christianisme: à partir de la création, dit l'Apôtre, l'homme entrevoit et saisit en quelque sorte le Créateur, sa puissance éternelle et sa divinité, et cela avec une telle évidence qu'il se sait et se sent obligé à reconnaître Dieu et à lui rendre un culte, de sorte que négliger ce culte ou le pervertir dans l'idolâtrie est gravement coupable, pour tous et dans tous les temps.

Ce n'est point ce que dit l'éthique dont Nous parlons. Elle ne nie pas, sans plus, les concepts et les principes moraux généraux (bien que parfois elle s'approche fort d'une semblable négation) mais elle les déplace du centre vers l'extrême périphérie. Il peut arriver que souvent la décision de la conscience leur corresponde. Mais ils ne sont pas, pour ainsi dire, une collection de prémisses, desquelles la conscience tire les conséquences logiques dans le cas particulier, le cas d' "une fois." Non pas! Au centre se trouve le bien, qu'il faut actuer ou conserver, en sa valeur réelle et individuelle; par exemple, dans le domaine de la foi, le rapport personnel, qui nous lie à Dieu. Si la conscience sérieusement formée décidait que l'abandon de la foi catholique et l'adhésion à une autre confession mène plus près de Dieu, cette démarche se trouverait "justifiée," même si généralement elle est qualifiée de "défection dans la foi." —Ou encore, dans le domaine de la moralité, le don de soi corporel et spirituel entre jeunes gens. Ici la conscience sérieusement formée déciderait qu'à raison de la sincère inclination mutuelle conviennent les privautés du corps et des sens, et celles-ci, bien qu'admissibles seulement entre époux, deviendraient manifestations permises. —La conscience ouverte d'aujourd'hui déciderait ainsi parce que de la hiérarchie des valeurs elle tire ce principe que les valeurs de personnalité, étant les plus hautes, pourraient se servir des valeurs inférieures du corps et des sens ou bien les écarter, selon que le suggère chaque situation. —On a bien avec insistance prétendu que, justement d'après ce principe, en matière de droit des époux, il faudrait, en cas de conflit, laisser à la conscience sérieuse et droite des conjoints, selon les exigences des situations concrètes, la faculté de rendre directement impossible la réalisation des valeurs biologiques, au profit des valeurs de personnalité.

Des jugements de conscience de cette nature, si contraires qu'ils semblent au premier abord aux préceptes divins, vaudraient cependant devant Dieu, parce que, dit-on, la conscience sincère sérieusement formée prime devant Dieu-même le "précepte" et la loi."

Une telle décision est donc "active" et "productrive," non "passive" et "réceptrice" de la décision de la loi, que Dieu a écrite dans le coeur de chacun, et moins encore de celle du Décalogue, que le doigt de Dieu a écrite sur des tables de pierre, à charge pour l'autorité humaine de le promulguer et de le conserver.

*La Morale Nouvelle Eminemment Individuelle.*

L'éthique nouvelle (adaptée aux circonstances) disent ses auteurs, est éminemment "individuelle." Dans la détermination de conscience l'homme singulier se rencontre immédiatement avec Dieu et se décide devant Lui, sans l'intervention d'aucune loi, d'aucune autorité, d'aucune communauté, d'aucun culte ou confession, en rien et en aucune manière. Ici il y a seulement le je de l'homme et le Je du Dieu personnel; non du Dieu de la loi, mais du Dieu Père, avec qui l'homme doit s'unir dans l'amour filial. Vue ainsi, la décision de conscience est donc un "risque" personnel, selon la connaissance et l'évaluation propres, en toute sincérité devant Dieu. Ces deux choses, l'intention droite et la réponse sincère, sont ce que Dieu considère; l'action ne Lui importe pas. De sorte que la réponse peut être d'échanger la foi catholique contre d'autres principes, de divorcer, d'interrompre la gestation, de refuser obéissance à l'autorité compétente dans la famille, dans l'Eglise, dans l'Etat, et ainsi de suite. Tout cela conviendrait parfaitement à la condition de "majorité" de l'homme et, dans l'ordre chrétien, à la relation de filiation, qui, selon l'enseignement du Christ, nous fait prier "notre Père." Cette vue personnelle épargne à l'homme de devoir à chaque instant mesurer si la décision à prendre correspond aux paragraphes de la loi ou aux canons des normes et régles abstraites; elle le préserve de l'hypocrisie, d'une fidélité pharisaique aux lois; elle le préserve tant du scrupule pathologique, que de la légèreté ou du manque de conscience, parce qu'elle fait reposer sur le chrétien personnellement l'entière responsabilité devant Dieu. Ainsi parlent ceux qui prônent la "nouvelle morale."

*Elle Est en Dehors de la Foi et des Principes Catholiques.*

Sous cette forme expresse l'éthique nouvelle est tellement en dehors de la foi et des principes catholiques, que même un enfant, s'il sait son catéchisme, s'en rendra compte et le sentira. Il n'est pas difficile de reconnaître comment le nouveau système moral dérive de l'existentialisme, qui ou fait abstraction de Dieu, ou simplement le nie, et en tout cas remet l'homme à soi-même. Il peut se faire que les conditions présentes aient induit à tenter de transplanter cette "morale nouvelle" sur le terrain catholique, pour rendre plus supportable aux fidèles les difficultés de la vie chrétienne. De fait, à des millions d'entre eux sont demandés aujourd'hui, en un degré extraordinaire, fermeté, patience, constance et esprit de sacrifice, s'ils veulent demeurer intègres dans leur foi, soit sous les coups de la fortune, soit dans un milieu qui met à leur portée tout ce à quoi le coeur passionné aspire, tout ce qu'il désire. Or une telle tentative ne pourra jamais réussir.

*Les Obligations Fondamentales de la Loi Morale.*

On demandera comment la loi morale, qui est universelle, peut suffire, et même être contraignante dans un cas singulier, lequel en sa situation concrète est toujours unique et d' "une fois." Elle le peut et elle le fait, parce que justement à cause de son universalité la loi morale comprend nécessairement et "intentionnellement" tous les cas particuliers, dans lesquels ses concepts se vérifient. Et dans des cas très nombreux elle le fait avec une logique si concluante, que même la conscience du simple fidèle voit immédiatement et avec pleine certitude la décision à prendre.

Ceci vaut spécialement des obligations négatives de la loi morale, de celles qui exigent un ne-pas-faire, un laisser-de-côté. Mais nullement de celles-là seules. Les obligations fondamentales de la loi morale se basent sur l'essence, la nature de l'homme et sur les rapports essentiels, et valent donc partout où se retrouve l'homme; les obligations fondamentales de la loi chrétienne, pour autant qu'elles excèdent celles de la loi naturelle, se basent sur l'essence de l'ordre surnaturel constitué par le divin Rédempteur. Des rapports essentiels entre l'homme, entre les conjoints, entre les parents et les enfants, des rapports essentiels de communauté dans la famille, dans l'Eglise, dans l'Etat, il résulte, entre autres choses, que la haine de Dieu, le blasphème, l'idolâtrie, la défection de la vraie foi, la négation de la foi, le parjure, l'homicide, le faux témoignage, la calomnie, l'adultère et la fornication, l'abus du mariage, le péché solitaire, le vol et la rapine, la soustraction de ce qui est nécessaire à la vie, la frustration du juste salaire (cfr. Iac, 5,4) l'accaparement des vivres de première nécessité et l'augmentation injustifiée des prix, la banqueroute frauduleuse, les manoeuvres de spéculation injustes—tout cela est gravement interdit par le Législateur divin. Il n'y a pas à examiner. Quelle que soit la situation individuelle, il n'y a d'autre issue que d'obéir.

Du reste Nous opposons à l'"éthique de situation" trois considérations ou maximes. La première: Nous concédons que Dieu veut premièrement et toujours l'intention droite; mais celle-ci ne suffit pas. Il veut aussi oeuvre bonne. Une autre: il n'est pas permis de faire le mal afin qu'il en résulte un bien (cfr. Rom, 3,8). Mais cette éthique agit—peut-être sans s'en rendre compte—d'après le principe que la fin sanctifie les moyens. La troisième: il peut y avoir des situations, dans lesquelles l'homme et spécialement le chrétien, ne saurait ignorer qu'il doit sacrifier tout, même sa vie, pour sauver son âme. Tous les martyrs nous le rappellent. Et ceux-ci sont fort nombreux en notre temps même. Mais le mère des Macchabées et ses fils, les saintes Perpétue et Félicité malgré leurs nouveaux-nés, Maria Goretti et des milliers d'autres, hommes et femmes, que l'Eglise vénère, auraient-ils donc, contre la "situation" inutilement ou même à tort encouru la mort sanglante? Non certes, et ils sont, dans leur sang, les témoins les plus exprès de la vérité, contre la "nouvelle morale."

*Le Problème de la Formation de la Conscience.*

La où il n'y a pas de normes absolument obligatoires, indépendantes de toute circonstance ou éventualité, la situation "d'une fois" en son unicité requiert, il est vrai, un examen attentif pour décider quelles sont les normes à appliquer et en quelle manière. La morale catholique a toujours et abondamment traité ce problème de la formation de la propre conscience avec examen préalable des circonstances du cas à décider. Tout ce qu'elle enseigne offre une aide précieuse aux déterminations de conscience, tant théoriques que pratiques. Qu'il suffise de citer les exposés, non dépassés de S. Thomas sur le vertu cardinale de prudence et les vertus qui s'y rattachent. (St. Th.2a 2ae p.a 47-57). Son traîté montre un sens de l'activité personnelle et de l'actualité, qui contient tout ce qu'il y a de juste et de positif dans l'"éthique selon la situation," tout en évitant ses conclusions et déviations. Il suffira donc au moraliste moderne de continuer dans le même ligne, s'il veut approfondir de nouveaux problèmes.

L'éducation chrétienne de la conscience est bien loin de négliger la personnalité, même celle de la jeune fille et de l'enfant, et de juguler son initiative. Car toute saine éducation vise à rendre l'éducateur peu à peu inutile et l'éduqué indépendant entre les justes limites. Et cela vaut aussi dans l'éducation de la conscience par Dieu et l'Eglise: son but est, comme le dit l'Apôtre (Eph. 4,13; cfr. 4, 14) l' "homme parfait, à la mesure de la plénitude d'âge du Christ," donc l'homme majeur, qui a aussi le courage de la responsabilité. Il faut seulement que cette maturité se situe au juste plan! Jésus-Christ reste le Seigneur, le Chef et le Maître de chaque homme individuel, de tout âge et de tout état, par le moyen de son Eglise en laquelle il continue d'agir. Le chrétien, pour sa part, doit assumer la grave et grande fonction de faire valoir dans sa vie personnelle, dans sa vie professionnelle, et dans la vie sociale et publique, autant qu'il dépend de lui, la vérité, l'esprit et la loi du Christ. C'est cela la morale catholique, et elle laisse un vaste champ libre à l'initiative et à la responsabilité personnelle du chrétien.

*Les Dangers pour la Foi de la Jeunesse.*

Voila ce que nous voulions vous dire. Les dangers pour la foi de notre jeunesse sont aujourd'hui extraordinairement nombreux. Chacun le savait et le sait, mais votre mémoire est particulièrement instructif à ce sujet. Toutefois Nous pensons que peu de ces dangers sont aussi grands et aussi lourds de conséquences que ceux que la "nouvelle morale" fait courir à la foi. Les égarements où conduisent de telles déformations et de tels amollissements des devoirs moraux, lesquels découlent tout naturellement de la foi, mèneraient avec le temps à la corruption de la source même. Ainsi meurt la foi.

*Deux Conclusions.*

De tout ce que Nous avons dit sur la foi, Nous tirerons donc deux conclusions, deux directives que Nous voulons vous laisser en terminant pour qu'elles orientent et animent toute votre action et toute votre vie de chrétiennes vaillantes.

La première—la foi de la jeunesse doit être une foi priante. La jeunesse doit apprendre à prier. Que ce soit toujours dans la mesure et en la forme qui répondent à son age. Mais toujours en ayant conscience que sans la prière il n'est pas possible de demeurer fidèle à la foi.

La seconde—la jeunesse doit être fière de sa foi et accepter qu'il lui en coûte quelque chose; elle doit dès la première enfance s'accoutumer à faire des sacrifices pour sa foi, à marcher devant Dieu en droiture de conscience, à révérer ce qu'Il ordonne. Alors elle croîtra comme d'elle-même dans l' amour de Dieu.

Que la charité de Dieu, la grâce de Jésus-Christ et la participation du Saint-Esprit (cfr. 2 Cr. 13,13) soient avec vous toutes, Nous vous le souhaitons avec la plus paternelle affection. Et pour vous la témoigner, de tout Notre coeur Nous vous donnons, à chacune de vous et à vos familles, à votre mouvement, à tous ses rameaux dans le monde entier, à toutes vos compagnes qui y adhèrent, la Bénédiction Apostolique.

Epilogue

# THE CASE AGAINST SITUATION ETHICS

*Morality and Situation Ethics* was published as *True Morality and its Counterfeits* in 1955. Its purpose was to render a critical examination of a body of thought which was ". . . not a philosophically formulated theory, but rather an intellectual movement, finding its expression in several youth organizations and in literature . . ." (p. 11)

Today, this book has gained new actuality through the fact that *Situation Ethics* is no longer to be found only in literary books which attempt to show how unsatisfactory the interpretation of traditional morality has often been in the past. Finding its champion in Mr. Fletcher's *Situation Ethics,* it now takes the form of a full-fledged attack on traditional morality.

Calling itself the "new morality," to benefit from the rich advantages granted by fashion, it claims in fact to be the one, authentic interpretation of the Gospel. Simultaneously it recognizes its indebtedness to Bentham (p. 95) who (very much to his own surprise), turns out to play a decisive role in Christian morality, thanks to his strategic principle: "The greatest good for the greatest number."

According to Mr. Fletcher, there are three basic types of ethics (later, in the same work, he claims that all ethics are eudemonistic. p. 96): the legalistic, the antinomian, and the golden mean: situation ethics.

Antinomian Ethics is rapidly described as "anarchic," "unprincipled" (p. 23).

Before starting a discussion of Mr. Fletcher's presentation of legalistic ethics, it is imperative to remark that he makes no distinction between moral laws, and positive divine laws, and further confuses the latter with state laws.

As these distinctions were crucial to traditional ethics (which Mr. Fletcher identifies without more ado with "legalistic" ethics), his presentation labors under a double equivocation.

His presentation of legalistic morality could be summarized as follows: it is a morality subjected to prefabricated laws of conduct that sacrifice the spirit to the letter of the law; it is one which is cold, impersonal and being committed to rules shows little concern for persons. Moreover, it is an ethic that has a ready made answer to all ethical difficulties, and caters to mediocrity by minimizing obligations. To quote Mr. Fletcher, legalistic ethics tells you "how much you must do, and no more" (p. 82).

After presenting legalistic ethics in this light, it is not surprising that Mr. Fletcher will win the sympathies of his public and gain acceptance for his ethics of "freedom" and "love." No great knowledge of psychology is required in order to make people realize that prohibitions are usually unwelcome, and that freedom (whatever it may mean) is popular.

But it is imperative to state that Mr. Fletcher's presentation of legalistic ethics is biased, or more exactly speaking, dishonest; for it is a systematic caricature of traditional ethics. It is traditional ethics as interpreted by a bureaucratic and mediocre mind.

While telling us that legalistic ethics sacrifices the spirit to the letter (and if it were so, who would endorse such ethics?), Mr. Fletcher does not take any pain to explain what he means by letter and by spirit. (*Morality and Situation Ethics* has devoted a whole chapter to this all important topic.) In the intellectual twilight that his vagueness has created, it is easy for Mr. Fletcher to juggle away the real issue, and to substitute conclusions that he has had up his sleeve from the beginning of the discussion.

The same attitude is exemplified in Mr. Fletcher's rejection of legalistic ethics as being impersonal. Once again, no one in his right mind will give preference to an abstract principle over a person. But while repeatedly referring to God, Mr. Fletcher systematically forgets to mention that if certain "principles" are disregarded, this implies an offense of God, the Infinite Person. The real issue is therefore not whether persons should be sacrificed to principles, but rather whether God is more important than man.

The way is now free for *Situation Ethics*. "The situationist follows a moral law or violates it according to love's need" (*Situation Ethics*, p. 26).

Mr. Fletcher is capitalizing on the power that slogans have

gained in our society. Having taken his lesson from politicians whose success is proportionate to their ability to produce slogans at a moment's notice, Mr. Fletcher serves us rich dishes of the most popular ones.

Let us review some of them. The most outstanding one is that "men have come of age" (p. 153). This slogan is gaining currency for the simple reason that everyone loves to be told how mature he is. But a few remarks are in order here: a public declaration that one is mature is not enough to guarantee maturity. As a matter of fact, psychologists know well that it is typical of immature people to try to convince others (and themselves) how mature they are. The truly mature person does not talk about his maturity; he behaves maturely. This and this alone is the test of maturity.

Furthermore, what do we mean by a mature behavior? Everyone agrees that a child is immature, and because of his immaturity, he is given help by those taking care of him. This help is simply taken for granted, and the child does not reflect much about it.

The puberty crisis begins the very moment a child attains the unquestioned assurance that he has come of age. This critical stage is characterized by an unsound craving for independence, and a systematic refusal of help, particularly when it is needed.

Authentic maturity, on the contrary, far from being a parading of one's independence, is characterized by the fact that a person becomes capable of recognizing by himself when he stands in need of help. The mature person begs for help when he realizes he needs it.

Mr. Fletcher seems to imply that maturity brings about a liberation from all duties and obligations, except the one to love; but he fails to see that the immature person clamors for his rights and forgets his obligations, whereas the mature person recognizes the interdependence of rights and obligations and faces these freely.

For the sake of argument let us grant Mr. Fletcher that man has now come of age. The consequence then would be that men, instead of being forced to meet their obligations, would now meet them freely. But maturity can never mean that obligations cease to be obligatory.

Does Mr. Fletcher mean to say that men of the past were to

obey the Ten Commandments because they were immature, and that the same Ten Commandments cease to be binding for Twentieth century man, because he has come of age? But the peculiarity of maturity is that man must meet more obligations; not less.

Much as men will mature, they will never reach a state when they will cease to be creatures, that is, to be in a metaphysical position essentially linked to *obedience*.

Mr. Fletcher reasons that man's creatureliness leads to the triumph of relativity: "The concept of human creatureliness at the very heart of Christian ethics cries, 'Relativity'! in the face of all smug pretensions to truth and righteousness" (p. 46).

But it does not seem to occur to him that it is *precisely* on account of his creatureliness that man has absolute obligations toward God who, after all, is also a Person.

Mr. Fletcher's interpretation of relativity also calls for a critical examination. He claims that ". . . the most pervasive culture trait of the scientific era and of contemporary man is the relativism with which everything is seen and understood" (p. 44); and further: "No Twentieth century man of even average training will turn his back on the anthropological and psychological evidence for relativity in morals" (p. 76).

But is not Mr. Fletcher running a bit behind the times? Is he aware that contemporary man is slowly walking up to the inconsistencies created by relativism, and taking a critical look at what was blindly accepted twenty years ago? We need only mention Melvin Rader's book, *Ethics and the Human Community*,[1] in which this Twentieth century author univocally points to the shortcomings of ethical relativism.

Morever, Mr. Fletcher seems to base his unconditional acceptance of ethical relativism on the ground that "there are no universal laws held by all men everywhere at all times, no consensus of all men" (p. 76). But if truth is based upon universal consensus, *Situation Ethics* is doomed.

Words like "never," "always," "absolutely" are avoided like the plague by the situationist, Mr. Fletcher tells us. After stating this, however, Mr. Fletcher makes abundant use of them in his own way. He tells us that respecting life is a maxim, never a rule (p.

[1] Holt, Rinehart 1964

55); or he says: "never sentimentalize love" (p. 103). If we take this view point seriously, then we ought to see that Mr. Fletcher is a relativist only when it suits him, for he is in fact introducing all sorts of new absolutes, which are no less absolute than those he has been fighting.

He praises the relativity of ethics as giving one "far greater humility than ever emerged in the classical intellectual tradition" (p. 45). No doubt, an ethics teaching humility is more ethical than one failing to do so. But here again, a query is in order: Is humility in Mr. Fletcher's eyes absolute? Are there situations in which humility ever deserves blame? If humility is relative, then Mr. Fletcher is paying the new ethics a left-handed compliment. If it is absolute, then why does he insist that love alone is absolutely good?

No one can accuse Mr. Fletcher of being chary in quoting the Bible, but one can accuse him of carefully omitting those passages of this sacred Book which would militate against his interpretation of ethics. He does mention repeatedly that the two key commandments are the love of God and the love of neighbor, but he takes the precaution of not mentioning that Christ also said: "He who loves me, keeps my commandments." Elementary logic teaches one that it is quite possible that a person keep the commandments and yet fails to love God in his heart (this criticism could be leveled at the legalists in the bad sense of the term). But it is just as true to say that he who breaks the commandments does not love Christ. This is made clear if we recall the words Christ addressed to the rich young man:

"But if you wilt enter into life, keep the commandments."
He said to him, "Which?" And Jesus said,
"Thou shalt not kill,
Thou shalt not commit adultery,
Thou shalt not steal,
Thou shalt not bear false witness,
Honor thy father and mother,
and, Thou shalt love thy neighbor as thyself" (Mt. 19, 18-19)

This quotation sheds light upon the fact that Mr. Fletcher's interpretation of biblical sentences is fraught with difficulties.

The author of *Situation Ethics* proclaims that we live in an age of honesty. This is good news indeed, provided that there is more than a show of honesty in words. For the dishonest man is not the one failing to proclaim his honesty but rather the one who behaves dishonestly.

It essentially belongs to intellectual honesty to present another person's position with objectivity and accuracy. We have already seen that Mr. Fletcher's presentation of legalistic morality is biased. For example, he fails to mention that legalistic ethics has always recognized the legitimate role played by circumstances in the making of ethical decisions. He brushes off the point by mentioning "casuistry," but makes no effort to show that there is an essential difference between "murder" and "killing" (for instance in legitimate self-defense); between "suicide" and "sacrifice" (see for example his interpretation of Mother Maria's sacrifice of herself to save a Jewish girl, as being a case of *suicide,* p. 74). It is wrong to call these all important distinctions "pilpul" or "hairsplitting," for they show that if situations are not the only decisive factor in determining whether an act is right or wrong, they do play a decisive role in morality.

Mr. Fletcher also tells us that because we live in an age characterized by honesty, "no one should abide by a standard that is not his own."

Traditional wisdom has shown through the centuries that one of the greatest difficulties confronting man is to get to know himself. Who am I? is a question difficult to answer. Moreover, philosophers (we are particularly thinking of Augustine, Kierkegaard and Marcel) have pointed out the fact that there are various levels in each individual man, so much so that one and the same person can manifest deep traits and superficial ones, can be generous and nevertheless selfish, Marcel has characterized this duality as the conflict existing within each between his "moi" and his "je."

When Mr. Fletcher declares that no one should abide by a standard that is not his own, we should like to know what this means. Does it mean that a selfish man should continue to be selfish because "he is then true to himself."

Hypocrisy consists of trying to appear what one is not, but who would dare say that a man is dishonest if recognizing his selfishness, he strives to struggle against it?

Honesty does not mean to behave as one feels like behaving, but rather to behave as one knows one *should* behave. Another biblical quotation here is truly called for: Every man is a liar.

The assertion that modern man lives in a scientific age leads to similar difficulties and confusions. The strides made by modern science are so amazing that they seem to justify a boundless optimism. But life teaches one that just as defeats can be transformed into victories (maybe these are the most authentic victories), victories can also be turned into defeats. Greek wisdom has shown that when hubris sets in, a hero is about to meet his doom.

The fact that men are conquering space and are about to reach the moon, can create, indeed has created such a state of unhealthy self-assurance (one speaks today of the dangers of a "debilitating humility"), that defeat might be closer than we realize.

Today it is enough indeed to stick the label "scientific" on any theory, however wild, in order to have it gain unconditional (and uncritical) acceptance. Scientific as physics, chemistry and medicine may be, we live in an age that also accepts as "scientific" the speculations offered by anthropology, sociology, psychology, psychiatry, while failing to make a much called for distinction between what is "scientific" and what is "pseudo-scientific" in the approach as well as in the conclusions of these disciplines.

We live in a scientific age, but we also live in an age where fairy tales and charlatanism are gaining wide acceptance, because they are introduced under the title of scientific discoveries or scientific advances.

At any rate, we should expect objectivity, accuracy and a critical spirit from a scientific age. Instead of this, Mr. Fletcher admits that *Situation Ethics* implies ". . . first guessing, and (that) much of its decision-making work entails a frightful measure of doubt and uncertainty and opacity" (p. 154).

The intellectual disarray typified by Mr. Fletcher's book is actually the result of a series of basic confusions related to the very nature of ethics.

The first one is evidenced when Mr. Fletcher bluntly declares that "the very first question in all ethics is What do I want?" (p. 42). This is surprising indeed. For if this is the basis of ethics, one has every good reason to reject Mr. Fletcher's ethics of love as being precisely the very ethics one does not want. Aristippus of Cyrene answered the question "What do I want" by "Pleasure," and on the basis of his argumentation, Mr. Fletcher would have a difficult time to show the father of Hedonism that he is actually missing the crucial ethical question. This is "What should I do," and not "what do I want."

Equally misleading is Mr. Fletcher's blind acceptance of David Hume's dichotomy between "is" and "ought" statements.

He tells us, "It was David Hume who set out this elementary point in its enduring form for British and American thinking" (p. 49).

Hume is indeed right in telling us that the fact that, let us say, water is $H_2O$ does not entitle us to say that it should be so. But $H_2O$ is a neutral fact, and to limit our horizons to these facts is to look at the universe with blinders on — a very unscientific approach.

What Mr. Fletcher overlooks (and David Hume too, for that matter) is that there are other types of facts, which we can call "value-facts."

These are just as real as other facts, because they *are,* but they are loaded with value, and due to their value, make possible the step leading from *is* to *should.* Justice is good, therefore I should be just.

One of the deeply rooted prejudices of the Anglo-American world (for prejudices are regional, whereas truth is not), is that facts are *a definitione* restricted to the scientific, neutral universe. But whether something is a fact, should be determined by whether or not it exists, and not by whether or not it is subject to laboratory-verification.

Mr. Fletcher advocates an ethics based on love. But why should we love? Why should we accept this particular ethical approach, if the goodness of love is not recognized as a fact?

The book draws its glory from its praise of love as being the only valid commandment: "The ruling norm of Christian decision is love; nothing else" (p. 69).

This sounds Christian enough, but the difficulty lies in explaining the meaning of love.

Mr. Fletcher's analysis of love calls for our close attention because he claims it to be the very core of *Situation Ethics.*

In order to focus properly on this problem, we might recall that legalistic ethics has been attacked by Mr. Fletcher as being cold, abstract and impersonal. We have tried to show that these criticisms are actually leveled at a caricature of legalistic ethics, but a caricature that, unfortunately has found many adherents in the history of philosophy. For example, one could level severe criticisms at "legalists" (in the bad sense of the term), because they have interpreted love as an act of will, and stripped it of its affective warmth and plenitude.

One experiences considerable surprise upon discovering that after having criticized legalistic ethics for its coldness, one discovers that Mr. Fletcher himself reduces love to a sheer act of will. We quote:

"Erotic and philic love are emotional, but the
affective principle of Christian love is will,
disposition; it is an attitude, not feeling" (p. 79).

There is a very serious philosophical difficulty involved in this position, namely that whereas love is directed toward persons (I love *someone*), will can only be directed toward the realization of a state of fact; in other words, I cannot will a person; I can only will that such and such be realized. How then can love be an act of *will*? I can will to do good to my neighbor, without loving him, without charity. This has been expressed by St. Paul in Corinthians 1, 13: "... and if I have all faith so as to remove mountains, yet do not have charity, I am nothing. And if I distribute all my goods to feed the poor, and if I deliver my body to be burned, yet do not have charity, it profits me nothing."

Mr. Fletcher's definition of love is important because it tends to undermine his assertion that his exclusive concern is with persons.

But this is only one of the difficulties of Mr. Fletcher's position. He proceeds by telling us that whereas *eros* is essentially emotional and selfish (p. 94; p. 104) (without making any effort to show why an emotional experience must be associated with selfishness), *agape,* that is, Christian love, is actually "nothing but justice" (p. 87).

"Now we state it flatly and starkly so that there is no
mistaking what is said. Love — justice; justice — love" (p. 95).

But if there is absolute identity of justice and love, is not Mr.

Fletcher more legalistic than the bad legalists ever managed to be? He attacks legalism in the name of love, but then, by means of a remarkable inconsistency, reduces love to justice. Does one need much philosophical probing to find out that Christian love is more than justice? The Greeks based their ethics upon the notion of justice, and never claimed to go beyond it. But when Christ said: "A new commandment I give you, that you love one another. . . . (Jn. 13, 34), He made it clear that love implied more than the obligation of strict justice.

In spite of these difficulties, Mr. Fletcher cheerfully proceeds to proclaim that situation ethics is the ethics of love. He thereby seems to put the whole emphasis on moral values, as opposed to morally relevant values. But the next moment (for Mr. Fletcher's argumentation moves rapidly) he reduces love (or justice) to the doing of good works: Love is nothing but justice, which is nothing but the bringing about the greatest good for the greatest number.

"Hence it follows that in Christian situation ethics
nothing is worth anything in and of itself. It gains
its value only because it happens to help persons" (p. 59).

As a result, love (which before was characterized as an attitude) "is not something we have or are, it is something that we do" (p. 61). But it is not difficult to realize that love cannot be only an attitude, and the next moment be something that we do.

Nevertheless, this latter assertion has the great advantage of shedding light on Mr. Fletcher's authentic position: pragmatism in Christian garb.

The real hero of the work is Bentham's theory of the "greatest happiness for the greatest number," with the difference that Bentham's position is clear from the start, and lays no claim to being Christian; whereas Fletcher's position is so loaded with biblical quotations that he can deceive some people into believing that he has finally unveiled the authentic core of Christian morality.

This is true even when Mr. Fletcher has to twist biblical sentences in order to have them fit into his own interpretation.

Here are two striking examples:
"For my thoughts are not your thoughts, neither are my ways your ways, says the Lord" (Isaiah, 55-8). This sentence is inter-

preted by Mr. Fletcher as offering a sound foundation for the relativity of ethics.

Isaiah's message, instead of being interpreted as referring to that which is not revealed (for example why God permits certain things to happen), is now used to undermine God's very revelation (namely the Ten Commandments).

Still more amazing is Mr. Fletcher's free interpretation of the anointing at Bethany: "The issue (he tells us) is between impetuous, uncalculating, unenlightened sentimental love, in the woman's use of the costly ointment, and a calculating, enlightened love" (p. 97); and further: "If we take the story as it stands, Jesus was wrong and the disciples right" (p. 97).

From the point of view of pragmatism — the Apostles' point of view  Mary Magdalen's action constituted a waste. But there are considerations other than pragmatic ones, namely the glorification of God, and this is a concept systematically ignored by Mr. Fletcher.

He starts off by speaking of love of God and love of neighbor; he ends by forgetting God to such an extent that he can say: "... we *only* (italics mine) serve God by serving our neighbors" (p. 158).

Direct love of God, the glorification of God, the offense of God through sin, are notions which are so thoroughly forgotten in Mr. Fletcher's presentation that one cannot help marveling whether, in a clandestine fashion, Mr. Fletcher does not belong to the "God is dead movement." God's name appears constantly in *Situation Ethics,* but for all practical purposes, he is but a ghost, whose relationship to human decision is non-existent. He is neither glorified by authentic virtue, nor offended by vices and immoralities. The I-thou relationship between God and man is replaced by an anonymous relationship to the human community. It looks very much as if the help of IBM machines will soon be enlisted to guide one in making "ethical" decisions, by calculating with accuracy the action or actions likely to shower the most benefits on the human race.

The question remains: Is God dead or is man deaf?

ALICE VON HILDEBRAND

"In this day of situation ethics," continued the editorial, "there are too many people espousing a philosophy that lifts all restraints. There are too many people who promote a contextual concept that would deny the existence of laws of morality that exist in all situations . . . What we need today is not apologizers but apostles."

The von Hildebrands are such apostles and *Morality and Situation Ethics* could not be more timely.

# *Morality*
### AND
# *Situation Ethics*

DIETRICH VON HILDEBRAND'S works have become classics in his own lifetime. *Transformation in Christ* and *Liturgy and Personality* are key books in the broad field of Christian spirituality. *Not as the World Gives*, on the Third Order of St. Francis, *The Art of Living* and *Man and Woman*, were published by Franciscan Herald Press. The author was formerly professor of philosophy at Fordham University; he is a figure of worldwide reputation as a teacher and writer.

ALICE JOURDAIN VON HILDEBRAND came to the U.S. from her native Belgium in 1940. She is associate professor of philosophy at Hunter College, New York, speaks many languages and specializes in matters pertaining to existential thought. She has mastered her husband's philosophy and thought and has become his best collaborator.